Assholes Matter

The Effects of Criticism on Mental Health and the Organization

By

Richard K. Zwicky

Life is a voyage through knowledge.

In our journeys, we learn from both positive and negative experiences.

What we take from each helps shape the person we become

and the lessons we will teach others.

Thank you for taking the time to read this book.

I hope you enjoy it and that at least one tip will help you reduce workplace toxicity.

Copyright 2024, Richard K. Zwicky

All Rights Reserved

Table of Contents

Preamble to the 2nd Edition

Perspectives and Improvements

Welcome to the (Constructive) Criticism Club!

Congratulations! You've picked up a book that just might change the way you see work, feedback, and, well, people. Maybe you're here because you've been on the receiving end of some truly horrendous criticism (we're talking "constructive" feedback that left you questioning your career choices and your existence). Or perhaps you're the one delivering feedback and have noticed that your comments, despite the best intentions, occasionally land like a lead balloon. Either way, you're in the right place.

This book is here to help you navigate the messy, hilarious, and sometimes maddening world of workplace dynamics, the places where criticism, personalities, and emotions collide like bumper cars at a corporate carnival. But don't worry; it's not all chaos and confusion. Together, we'll uncover the secrets of using criticism as a tool for growth, transforming even the most awkward conversations into opportunities for connection and success.

You might think, Can't I just avoid criticism altogether? Wouldn't that be nice! Criticism is as inevitable in the workplace as awkward small talk at the coffee machine. But here's the thing: it doesn't have to be dreadful. In fact, when handled thoughtfully, it can make the difference between a stagnant team and one that thrives.

Criticism: The Gift No One Wants (Until They Do)

When most people encounter the term "criticism," they often feel defensive, picturing accusations, red marks, and well-meaning advice that seems as useful as a screen door on a submarine. However, effective criticism isn't about diminishing someone or highlighting flaws for amusement. Instead, it focuses on uplifting, clarifying, and providing a way forward.

Think of constructive criticism like a good map. It doesn't tell you, "Wow, you're lost, loser!" and then leave you stranded. Instead, it says, "Here's where you are, and here's how to get to where you want to be."

1

This book is here to help you learn how to understand, assess, and create feedback that turns criticism into a fun treasure hunt instead of a daunting journey through Mordor.

You might have experienced the unique joy (or the occasional frustration) of receiving feedback from one of "those" bosses. You know the ones the ones who think "constructive criticism" means highlighting every little flaw with the delicacy of a bull in a china shop. Equally useful, you may have worked for a boss who showered you with compliments like candy but skipped over any meaningful commentary or practical advice. These bosses can leave you wondering if they're just being polite when they gaslight you, if they pay any attention to your work, or if they even noticed you used Comic Sans in the annual report!

The truth is, most people never learned how to give great feedback, and for various reasons, most of us struggle to receive it, too. That's where this book comes in. By the time you're done reading, you'll understand:

> - How to deliver feedback that lands like a high-five instead of a slap.
> - How to receive criticism without spiraling into self-doubt or plotting your resignation.
> - How to foster a workplace culture where criticism is constructive and not a grenade.

You might be wondering; *You mean criticism doesn't need to sting?*

Absolutely! It's a fact that great workplaces flourish when team members share feedback in positive, constructive ways. Sadly, many managers aren't aware of how to approach this effectively. But guess what? You're already on the right track! If you aspire to earn that promotion, mastering the art of managing people starts with embracing outstanding communication skills, particularly the ability to provide constructive criticism! We all deserve criticism occasionally. Constructive criticism uplifts us to do better. But unfortunately, most people use criticism to, well, criticize and demean. That's abuse, and it needs to stop!

No matter your role; be it manager, team member, or anything in between, you have the potential to be a wonderful leader! The way you handle feedback can truly shape your relationships, so why not embrace the opportunity to excel at it? After all, we all know that navigating people can be quite a challenge, so let's make it as smooth as possible!

Creating a culture of constructive criticism not only enhances individual relationships and team performance, but it also strengthens connections, fosters trust, and sparks innovation. When people feel secure in giving and receiving feedback, they're much more inclined to take risks, explore new ideas, and learn from their experiences. That's truly where the magic unfolds!

Sometimes, human interactions can feel a bit awkward! One of the wonderful ways to ease that tension is through some light-hearted humor. When we can share a laugh about ourselves and our little slip-ups, it helps everyone feel more at ease, fostering an atmosphere where even the toughest conversations don't seem so daunting.

By the end of this book, I hope you'll have gained new perspectives, skills, insights, and strategies to help you:

- Turn even the most challenging feedback sessions into productive, positive conversations.
- Identify and navigate toxic behaviors before they derail your team's morale.
- Cultivate a culture of mutual respect and continuous learning, where feedback is a source of inspiration, not anxiety.

Hopefully, you will recognize some of your own behaviors, as well as those of others you know, and that this perspective aids in deepening your understanding of how you both give and receive feedback.

This isn't just a book about work; it's about people and their potential. It's all about how we can inspire ourselves and each other to shine. Constructive criticism is just one part of the journey, but it's an important one that weaves together leadership, teamwork, personal growth, and success. As you hone your own skills, I hope you'll embrace your mistakes, learn to laugh at any missteps, and take a moment to celebrate your victories. If you do, you'll find that even small changes in how we communicate can spark amazing transformations.

When you embrace feedback as a tool for connection and progress, you improve your work and home environment and contribute to a culture where everyone has the chance to shine. That's a pretty amazing legacy to leave behind.

So, are you ready to trade the dread of criticism for curiosity, understanding, and growth?

That's a rhetorical question of course…. Who wouldn't want more personal peace and accomplishment?

So, let's get started: the journey to better relations at work and home begins with one constructive conversation at a time.

Allow me to begin with a confession: Sometimes, I, too, can be an asshole!

However, I'm not insensitive, and when I occasionally and unintentionally interact carelessly with another person and come across as rude, I'm mortified. Whether in my professional or personal life, if I respond poorly to someone, I've made a mistake, and I apologize.

Managers and leaders need to be acutely aware of how their words and tone of voice are heard at work. When you are in a position of authority over others, you must comport yourself to a higher standard. Whether intentional or note, being rude is a form of bullying, and no form of abuse should ever be accepted in a healthy organization

It's disheartening when we observe people in positions of authority who are aware of their inappropriate behavior and still choose to deny it. Rather than offering an apology, they try to dismiss the feelings of others, sometimes even claiming that their actions are acceptable. Sadly, this can lead to even more hurt, as some even insist that those affected are overly sensitive.

I've observed this behavior both in professional settings and personal interactions, particularly in the dynamics between spouses and others. Challenges faced at home often translate into workplace relationships.

To minimize toxicity in the workplace, it's essential to improve how we manage difficult individuals. If managers and leaders fail to handle criticism and its delivery wisely, we may not recognize how negativity, ineffective communication, and a deficiency in accountability can undermine organizational culture, productivity, and morale.

It's completely natural to feel a bit uneasy when we hear that someone is going to share feedback or criticism. Most people's first response is to feel a wave of dread washing over us, as we anticipate a personal attack. However, criticism can be a positive experience! When shared in a constructive way, it is what helps us grow. Interestingly, the word "critique," which is the root of criticism, actually means a thoughtful judgment or evaluation of both the strengths and weaknesses of something. Embracing this perspective can make all the difference!

Constructive criticism should acknowledge a person's strengths and commendable qualities while also addressing areas for improvement. Yet merely pinpointing a shortcoming isn't enough. To ensure the criticism is productive, it must lay out a clear plan, including specific milestones for improvement.

This book examines how to effectively manage criticism, both constructive and negative, while also highlighting the impact of toxic behaviors in the workplace. It provides practical strategies for leaders and teams to identify, mitigate, and convert these toxic dynamics into a positive culture characterized by constructive feedback, resilience, collaboration, and respect.

Without goalposts, no one can ever score!

If we don't understand what the standards are that we are expected to adhere to, we can't meet expectations, can we?

Now, let's return to the concept of Assholes and the role they play in criticism, toxicity, and corporate culture.

Let's begin with a truth we can all acknowledge: Assholes really come in all shapes and sizes. The statement might make you chuckle, but I hope it also encourages some reflection, which is always a positive step!

One of the toughest types to deal with are those weak-minded narcissists who crave attention and try to dodge accountability for the hurt they've caused. I've encountered a few who, despite knowingly causing pain to others, ironically ask, "Why is this happening to me?"

Rather than resolve the problems their toxic behavior created, these individuals attempt to gaslight others into believing they were the wronged party. While repugnant, their behavior reflects unaddressed issues related to the toxic nature of their upbringing. Later in the book, we will delve into managing these types of people.

I've had a lot of time to think about updating this book, and this update is long overdue. In fact, the update was required the moment I published it, and this is my mea culpa.

When I wrote "Assholes Matter" a year ago, I had assembled a series of thematically similar articles that I had written. I had not intended to publish the book immediately, but I wanted a copy for myself because reading a printed copy gives me a better perspective on editing.

I meant to order myself a few copies to use for editing, but instead, I published, got distracted (as those of us blessed with ADHD are prone to have happen), and left it live!

So now, months later, I am finally returning to fix my mistake.

A funny thing happened along the way...

When I chose the title for this book, I figured it would be provocative, and the double meaning of 'Assholes Matter' relative to the topic of criticism would cause people to stop and think. I didn't think it all the way through though...!

The first day I had a physical copy of my book, I was in a coffee shop, and while I was standing at the counter waiting to enjoy my coffee, I chatted with the person next to me. After a brief conversation, she glanced at my book and said, *"They do, and you should get to know mine."*

Amazingly, this was not a one-time occurrence, and it didn't just happen to me! When I told friends about what had happened, they got copies and shared similar experiences!

I never imagined that my book would become a conversation starter or used as a pick-up tool in coffee shops, restaurants, and lounges!

Needless to say, the book has provided people with value beyond what's between the sheets (of paper)

~

This book was written to be helpful to others who are struggling to deal with difficult personalities, or even to come to terms with their own challenges. This book is based on my experience dealing with all sorts of characters. Most people I have worked with were not Assholes. In fact, I've been fortunate to have dealt with overwhelmingly wonderful people throughout my life and career.

There's no finger-pointing in this book. But if there were, I'd point at myself more often than anyone else. I wish I had learned more about these issues sooner so that I could have avoided making mistakes and also helped others better manage conflict and to prevent them from becoming toxic.

By sharing my perspectives and insights, I hope to help each of you explore the impact that criticism, both constructive and toxic, has on your lives, and helps you make positive contributions to you organization's culture.

The book is a series of essays tied together by one key theme. Each chapter offers standalone insights on specific aspects of criticism, feedback, and organizational behavior. To address the question of how criticism affects organizations, the book discusses the necessity of constructive criticism, empathy in leadership, managing the ripple effect of toxic behavior, and fostering organizational cultures that encourage growth and mutual respect.

Together, we will recognize that everyone has the capacity to grow and improve, and by embracing our flaws with humility and humor, we can create healthier, more compassionate workplaces.

I hope these insights will help you avoid many of the mistakes we all make.

Introduction
Building Strong Organizations

Being demanding does not require anyone to be rude. It is not hard to be both demanding and constructive while remaining respectful. So, why do many people find it difficult to remain respectful and constructive when dealing with others?

The answer is simple: Humans are wonderfully complex creatures with remarkable talents and fundamental flaws. Within each of us resides an unfinished masterpiece. We are like unfinished works of art, and the wisest among us never ceases to learn or improve.

To reach our potential, we need to open our minds and accept guidance from a wide array of mentors who gently expose our weaknesses, soften our rough edges, and guide us along. Interpersonal relationships are among the many skills we improve.

Let's begin our journey by exploring the subtle but pervasive influence of negative behaviors on organizational culture.

> *Have you ever been inspired by a leader who made navigating people's quirks*
> *feel like solving an amusing, real-life puzzle?*

Great leadership is about more than just setting high expectations. It's rooted in embracing self-sacrifice to create an environment that uplifts.

Leadership calls for high standards, but being demanding doesn't mean being disrespectful. It's essential to practice constructive and respectful leadership to foster a positive team environment, even though maintaining this balance can be tricky.

So, what makes maintaining that proper balance a challenge for some people? The complexity of human nature is a big factor. Each of us is a unique "work-in-progress," full of talent and potential but also with little quirks that, if not managed well, can impact our professional lives.

Reaching our potential is all about nurturing our skills and recognizing areas we can improve. Constructive feedback plays a crucial role in this journey, allowing us to smooth out our rough edges and enhance our workplace relationships.

It's important to remember that negative behaviors can quickly and quietly influence our organizational culture. By grasping how personal issues can lead to workplace conflicts, and how unresolved challenges can increase stress among teams, we empower leaders to tackle the core issues that may be creating tension.

Criticism can be a powerful tool. When given thoughtfully, it encourages growth. But if mishandled, it fosters toxicity. For those who wrestle with personal struggles, the art of giving and receiving feedback respectfully can be a challenge.

Without proper support to help us address our weaknesses, individuals may opt for the simplest route, and in doing so, inadvertently add to workplace stress. Although everyone makes mistakes, shying away from the difficult conversations required to discuss mistakes so as to avoid upsetting others is a far greater error. Avoidance leads to increased stress throughout the organization.

Stress affects us all, and some reports indicate that over 80% of doctor visits stem from stress-related causes. U.S. businesses lose over $300 billion annually due to stress-induced absenteeism and diminished productivity.

Being in a leadership position comes with its own set of challenges, and managing stress and emotional responses is crucial. A stressed manager who cannot contain frustration may unintentionally spread negativity within the team. The good news is that leaders can absolutely change this behavior, which is key not only for their own happiness but also for the team's overall growth.

Feedback, particularly constructive criticism, is a powerful catalyst for growth. Delivered mindfully, it reveals blind spots and illuminates paths for improvement. Accepting constructive feedback with an open mind is a vital skill that also enhances one's ability to deliver it compassionately.

As George Matthew Adams observed,

> *"There is no such thing as a 'self-made man.' We are made up of thousands of others. Everyone who has ever done a kind deed for us or spoken one word of encouragement to us has entered into the makeup of our character and of our thoughts, as well as our success."*

Adams was right, our successes are built upon the support and encouragement of others. Just as the greatest athletes in sports require teammates to help them increase their point totals, we all need constructive interactions to drive personal growth.

Similarly, meaningful growth requires constructive exchanges with others. These interactions help us shape our skills, mindset, and resilience.

While we all strive for harmony, it's completely normal to encounter conflict along the way. In fact, these moments can teach us so much—especially if we keep an open mind and stay self-aware. We begin learning about conflict early in life, starting at home, continuing through school, and later in our careers, where managing conflict truly becomes an essential skill.

Some conflicts can be quite constructive, like when two teams passionately discuss the best ideas for a project. In organizations that embrace open discussions, differing opinions spark creativity and improve open communication.

Constructive criticism plays a vital role in ongoing development. When given effectively, it provides insight; when conveyed ineffectively, it can weaken. Leaders need to emphasize respectful and constructive communications to stop toxicity from entering the workplace, undermining culture, and harming credibility.

Successful organizations thrive when their leaders embrace the power of respect, uphold high standards, and foster constructive interactions. When leaders actively seek input, value everyone's contributions, and show genuine appreciation, they inspire loyalty and dedication. These thoughtful gestures reassure team members that their hard work truly matters, helping to build a strong foundation of trust and engagement.

Feedback becomes truly impactful when it offers clear, actionable suggestions. Leaders who take the time to provide specific context for improvement show genuine concern and encourage growth. By focusing on behaviors instead of character, leaders maintain dignity while encouraging development and change.

Creating a healthy workplace is all about encouraging open communication that truly supports employee well-being.

When employees feel disrespected or unsupported, stress can build up, which often leads to burnout, anxiety, and other health challenges. By putting in place policies that foster open communication and prioritize mental health, such as offering confidential counseling services, we can make a big difference in reducing workplace stress and nurturing a happier, healthier workforce engagement.

To genuinely improve organizational culture, leaders need to live out the values they advocate. Open and honest communication, along with accountability, are crucial. Leaders should solicit feedback on their own work and recognize the constructive contributions of others publicly. They also must deal with harmful criticism promptly, and manage others by consistently demonstrating the behaviors they wish to see.

Constructive feedback serves a crucial function in the actualization of both individual and organizational potential.

Creating a culture of constructive feedback is an exciting journey, especially in established organizations. Changes to long-standing communication habits often encounter unexpected resistance, as people may feel that constructive feedback is actually criticism. Involving employees in helping shape the new culture can being with participation in the development of any new communication guidelines and accountability measures will help everyone feel valued and invested in the outcome.

The cultural transformation of an organization often takes a winding path, and we should expect more than a few bumps along the way. By demonstrating resilience, focus, and perseverance, leaders ensure the organization maintains course. By celebrating the small victories as other embrace their ideals, they also keep the momentum going during tough times. While adopting a culture based on constructive feedback may be uncomfortable for some, doing so lays a wonderful foundation for personal and collective growth and innovation.

It's important for everyone to share the same perspective and embrace the idea that cultural change in an organization can't be achieved through a memo alone; it requires everyone's buy-in and involvement.

When considering your organization or your future organization's cultural direction, you must approach the issues mindfully in ways that include the following ongoing steps:

> - Regularly seeking feedback from their team members, demonstrating vulnerability and openness to constructive criticism. This sets the tone that feedback is valued at all levels.

- Publicly acknowledge and reward employees who provide constructive feedback, even if it challenges the status quo. This reinforces that speaking up is not only safe but celebrated.

- Address instances of toxic criticism swiftly and equitably. Leaders must hold themselves and others accountable for adhering to the new communication norms.

- Model the desired behaviors in all interactions, from one-on-one conversations to company-wide communications. Employees take cues from leadership on what is truly valued.

- Invest time and resources into training and support for all employees to develop constructive feedback skills. Change requires more than good intentions.

- Monitor progress, celebrate wins, and course-correct as needed. Leaders must sustain focus and commitment to embed the new culture.

The key to success is to solicit honest input, communicate findings transparently, and then to act on the insights. Sustaining the changes requires authenticity in the efforts, as well as vigilant attention to opportunities for continuous improvement.

It's simpler to start fresh when building a new organization, but existing entities can and must adapt as well. Cultivating a culture of constructive feedback requires building skills and habits across the entire organization.

Building a culture of constructive feedback is a journey that takes dedication, but the rewards are truly amazing! When feedback is given in a supportive and understanding way, it creates an atmosphere of trust and psychological safety, helping everyone perform at their best.

Leaders who foster this kind of environment empower their organizations and teams to shine. By leading by example and offering thoughtful guidance, leaders open the door to shared growth, resilience, and lasting success for everyone involved.

Leadership is about fostering respect and connection, creating environments where every individual feels valued and empowered to grow.

Building Healthy Organizations
The People Challenges of Leadership

Every business leader faces challenges related to products, marketing, branding, finances, operations, and, most fundamentally, people. Regardless of industry or company size, criticism and conflict inevitably emerge in the workplace. When left unaddressed, these issues become more pervasive as organizations grow and more employees join.

> *Have you ever dealt with someone whose idea of 'team-building' was to criticize everyone else's work into compliance, or until they quit?*

> *or*

> *Have you ever seen a team so committed to creating a healthy workplace that universal trust is obvious to all?*

A healthy workplace is built upon a culture that values respect, clear communication, and accountability. Effective, constructive criticism is crucial for growth and improvement. Creating a culture that welcomes fair and constructive feedback necessitates a thoughtful approach and managers who reflect the core values of respect, accountability, and honesty.

In contrast, poorly delivered criticism quickly and severely damages team morale and unity. When feedback is received in a negative light, staff productivity declines as they become resentful toward both the individual who delivered it and the company for allowing it to happen. Eventually, the disaffected will begin to search for alternative employment.

Even a single disenchanted employee can create a toxic work environment for those around them. As this behavior persists, it spreads, leading to further demotivation, detachment, and declining productivity among staff.

A 2022 MIT study analyzed over 500 U.S. companies and found that organizations struggling with widespread toxicity experienced 31% lower productivity and 44% higher voluntary turnover than industry benchmarks. The study estimated that annual financial losses due to reduced output and turnover exceeded $23 billion across the companies surveyed. These figures underscore the profound impact that toxic cultures and mishandled criticism can have on operations, retention, and profits.

Leaders and managers must recognize that a toxic work environment harms not only employees but also their families, as work pressures spill into personal lives and affect relationships.

Generally, employees come to work eager to contribute. In time, their contributions give them a sense of accomplishment that combine to shape= their professional identity. Yet, despite people's dependency on their jobs for their professional self-esteem, a 2021 Gallup study revealed that only 20% of U.S. employees strongly agreed with the statement that their performance is managed in a way that motivates them to excel.

For 80% of employees, constructive feedback is either lacking or entirely absent. This striking statistic highlights an enormous problem and opportunity: with appropriate support and guidance, productivity and job satisfaction could be significantly enhanced.

Gallup's report also found that over half of surveyed employees felt they didn't receive sufficient praise or recognition for good work. Without clear and frequent guidance, it's difficult for employees to know what success looks like!

People are naturally social, and we all thrive on feeling respected and appreciated by those around us. To keep our talented individuals engaged and motivated, it's essential that workplace cultures cater to this fundamental human need. When employees don't receive recognition and praise, they might find it challenging to feel satisfied in their roles.

In the past, feedback in the workplace often flowed from the top down in structured organizations, which could sometimes create a sense of anxiety. This is because managers were seen as the authority, and employees often felt like they had a subordinate role.

Nowadays, management practices have shifted to embrace the importance of two-way communication, recognizing that collaboration among all team members is vital to achieving success. Today's managers are genuinely eager to hear from their staff and offer helpful, encouraging feedback, fostering an inclusive atmosphere where everyone's contributions truly matter.

Two-way communication allows both staff and management to learn and supports the notion that mistakes are vital learning opportunities. While mistakes are inevitable, constructive feedback provides the guidance necessary for learning and growth.

A 2022 Forbes survey of more than 1,500 corporations revealed that 68% of large companies now report having a "non-hierarchical workflow." This trend toward flatter, more transparent leadership structures highlights the importance of credibility, collaboration, and accountability in staff and manager promotions and evaluations. While many companies still maintain traditional reporting structures, the expectations for managers have (thankfully) evolved.

Former U.S. President Barack Obama once remarked, "If you've got a business, you didn't build that. Somebody else made that happen." While some independent-minded business owners may find this perspective challenging, it speaks to the truth that no one achieves success alone. For example, in football, a wide receiver's success depends on teammates creating opportunities for the quarterback to pass them the ball so they can make the play.

In a similar vein, it's important to recognize that there are no truly "self-made" successes. For example, countless individuals played a part in shaping Jeff Bezos' fortune at Amazon. Likewise, business failures typically don't arise from the choices of just one person; they always result from a variety of factors. However, it's common for people to assign both credit and blame to single individuals. This tendency can often lead leaders to feel that "it's lonely at the top."

To truly inspire the teams they assemble, a leader must take time to reflect on the unique value each team member contributes to the organization. While one individual may reap significant rewards from a successful venture, a great leader makes sure the whole team has what they need to thrive individually, allowing everyone to share in the collective success.

Business leaders are no different from anyone else. They are coaches, mentors, and individuals who bring unique skills and experience to their roles. Even star athletes like Michael Jordan and LeBron James rely on teamwork to achieve their records, underscoring that an individual's success often rests on a collective's efforts.

The same principle works both ways! Just as we recognize that leaders shouldn't bear all the credit for an organization's successes, we must also recognize that they shouldn't take all the blame when things don't go as planned. Using another sports analogy, take a goalie in a hockey game. If they miss a save, it's important to remember that the chance for the opposing team to shoot came from the collective failures of their teammates to prevent the shot. It's all about teamwork, and in winning or losing, everyone plays a role!

Refusing to acknowledge one's role in failures is also a missed opportunity for learning and growth, and creates unique stresses from inaction, preventing future growth.

A 2021 survey by the American Psychological Association found that over 80% of U.S. employees reported at least one workplace stressor, with inadequate staffing and unclear job expectations among the top issues. These challenges point to a basic need for improved communication and support networks.

Communication is the bedrock of successful relationships and reducing stress. Leaders must prioritize open communication channels between management and staff, enabling early identification and resolution of pain points. By actively listening and responding to criticism with empathy, managers set a foundation for mutual respect. Engagement surveys, regular team check-ins, anonymous feedback forms, and an open-door policy can all contribute to this effort.

For instance, Quip, a software company with around 200 employees, conducts quarterly surveys on factors affecting employee happiness, such as workload, career opportunities, and manager support. By regularly assessing and acting on these insights, Quip maintains an overall team satisfaction rating of over 90%.

Their commitment to employee experience explains Quip's strong growth and low turnover rates, highlighting the benefits of regularly soliciting feedback. Two-way feedback builds a positive culture; however, even well-intentioned feedback can backfire if it is poorly delivered.

Constructive criticism requires tact and actionable guidance. For example, a vague complaint about an "uncooperative attitude" should be reframed to pinpoint specific incidents where teamwork was lacking. Thoughtful critique can be challenging but is essential to nurturing a positive work environment.

Receiving criticism with appreciation is equally important. Both skills are learned over time and contribute to shared goals.

For leaders aiming to enhance their organization's culture, self-assessment is the first step. Understanding personal strengths and areas for growth underscores the importance of tailored feedback. Humans communicate in dominant styles, impacting how feedback is received; analytical personalities may prefer direct, evidence-based feedback, while relationship-focused individuals may value more supportive framing.

Leaders can reshape culture by modeling the behaviors they wish to see. However, creating lasting change requires humility, consistency, and courage. Leaders who embrace this challenge position their organizations for long-term success in retention, productivity, and innovation.

If leaders default to blame and negativity, staff will follow suit, fostering a toxic environment. Transformative change goes beyond good intentions; it requires skill-building and behavioral modeling.

Authentic, empowering workplace cultures are the ones that endure. Other organizations may find success temporarily but often struggle during turbulent times. In well-constructed organizations, leaders set a positive tone that defines norms for feedback, fostering potential, belonging, and growth for all stakeholders. This blueprint offers a promising path for organizations ready to support the people who make success possible.

A strong organization begins with a foundation of respect, collaboration, and shared purpose, ensuring every member feels part of a collective success story.

Factors Influencing Organizational Culture

It's all about us

Organizational culture is so much more than just a set of values written down or statements in a handbook—it's a vibrant, evolving force that touches every corner of an organization. This shared personality, shaped by values, beliefs, and norms, influences how employees see their roles, work together, and tackle challenges. As organizations grow and adapt to changes around them, it's important for their cultures to evolve too, ensuring they stay relevant, meaningful, and supportive.

Culture underlies every aspect of an organization, shaping decision-making, employee dynamics, and client connections. A healthy culture propels success by promoting engagement, increasing productivity, and cultivating loyalty. It can improve a company's standing, making it appealing to prospective employees, partners, and customers. In contrast, a detrimental culture may result in elevated turnover, reduced performance, and a tarnished reputation.

> *Have you ever worked in an office that was so toxic that it seemed like even the plants were searching for new jobs?*

> *or*

> *Have you ever worked in a place where the culture was so well balanced that you couldn't help but feel like you were part of creating greatness?*

Understanding the critical role of culture in shaping behavior and productivity allows us to identify the foundational components of workplace culture, including leadership styles, employee interactions, and internal policies. Implementing the right culture requires us to examine these components objectively, using constructive criticism to refine and improve the organization's cultural environment.

Constructive criticism, distinct from negative criticism, is a crucial feedback tool for fostering growth and maintaining a positive, adaptable workplace. Unlike criticism which is intended to demean, constructive feedback provides specific, actionable suggestions that support personal and professional development. Research by London and Smither (2002) in the *Journal of Management* demonstrated that when feedback is constructive, it enhances motivation, job satisfaction, and performance.

By offering clear and actionable feedback, managers will guide employees toward better performance and professional growth. Properly delivered, the lessons will also offer insights for personal growth that improve non-workplace relationships.

For example, Google's Project Oxygen, an internal study of their management practices, found that the most successful managers provided what they called "actionable feedback"—feedback that is specific, relevant, and offers a clear pathway for improvement. This feedback helps employees understand where to improve and how to do so.

> *We are all aware we can improve. Discovering what we need to improve is where our journey to personal growth begins. Knowing precisely which steps to take is the key we are all searching for.*

Constructive feedback is crucial. It helps us understand where we are in our life-long journey of improvement and fosters the environment required to build a positive organizational culture.

Effective constructive criticism is characterized by respect and empathy, targeting specific actions or results instead of individual traits. It cultivates a supportive atmosphere where feedback is seen as a chance for growth rather than punishment. This method encourages employees to embrace their development, nurturing a culture of ongoing learning improvement.

Constructive criticism fosters open communication, enhancing employees' feelings of being valued and understood. Research, such as Gallup's 2017 report, indicates that employees who receive consistent, constructive feedback exhibit higher engagement and productivity levels. Engaged employees, akin to motivated athletes, perform better and have a lower likelihood of departing from the organization, thus positively influencing overall organizational success.

The positive impact of constructive criticism extends beyond employee development; it also identifies and cultivates leadership potential. Employees who excel at providing constructive feedback are often seen as leaders—setting a positive example, fostering collaboration, and driving teams toward organizational goals.

Leadership's role in shaping and maintaining culture is essential. Leaders at every level must embody and demonstrate the organization's values through their actions. This involves making decisions with integrity, handling conflicts transparently and setting strategic directions that reinforce a positive culture. Leaders serve as role models, and their behavior, observed by others, profoundly influences the cultural tone of the organization.

An organization's policies and practices tangibly reflect its culture. Policies regarding work-life balance, continuous learning, and team collaboration communicate the values the organization upholds. These practices also provide a framework for expected behaviors, guiding employees in how they perform their roles and interact with others.

Just as an organization's current policies and practices define its culture, so does its history. Just consider the debates in the legislatures and courtrooms of the U.S.A. with regard to Founder's Intent, and how they should govern how Americans should govern their lives 250 years later.

An organization's Founding principles, past challenges, and successes create traditions and norms that often persist over time. Leaders who seek to change or evolve a culture must understand these historical elements, as they reveal deeply ingrained practices and values that shape the current culture.

Defining and embedding core values is a crucial first step in developing an organizational culture. Ideally, these values are based on growth principles and not the enrichment of a few. When an organization is created with the founder's gain as fundamental, toxicity is built into the system.

My high school's motto was "Non Nobis Solum," which means "not for ourselves alone." When we consider this belief with regards to structuring and managing an organization, we gain clarity and purpose on avoiding toxicity. This standard belief is integral to aligning the organization's vision, mission, guiding behaviors and decision-making at all levels.

Clear communication of these values ensures they are understood and embraced across the organization, often through hiring, evaluations, and everyday practices.

Effective communication is fundamental to sustaining a positive culture. Regular, open discussions about culture, values, and goals enable feedback, identify areas for improvement, and reinforce positive aspects. Inclusive communication channels allow all employees to access important messages and provide input, fostering a deeper sense of ownership and engagement with the organization.

Change is an inevitable, but it's also a challenge when developing culture. For many people, change of any type is scary. Thus, the first hurdle to overcome is their fear and bias against change, which drives their resistance to new policies and procedures, no matter how logical they may appear. Clear communication about the reasons for change and its alignment with organizational goals can alleviate skepticism. Involving employees in the change process, listening to their concerns, and valuing their input help foster a supportive environment.

Inconsistencies between stated values and observed behaviors will rapidly undermine cultural integrity, leading to disengagement among employees. When there's a disconnect between what the organization claims to value and what it practices, employees can become cynical. Addressing these inconsistencies requires honest self-assessment and a willingness to adjust policies, leadership practices, and behaviors to align with the desired culture.

Cultural inclusivity becomes increasingly important as organizations grow and diversify. Embracing a variety of cultural norms and values requires a holistic organizational commitment to inclusivity, especially in multinational settings. Effective leaders harness the unique strengths of diverse cultural backgrounds, using them to build bridges and promote a cohesive, respectful environment.

In some cultures, work is tightly intertwined with an individual's sense of personal identity, while in others, personal values and identity may take precedence over professional roles. This difference can create challenges, particularly when feedback is perceived as personal criticism.

In multinational organizations, leaders are required to bridge cultural gaps and foster an environment where that is sensitive to a much greater diversity of beliefs and perspectives and to ensure that all are valued and respected.

In North America, we tend to associate our work overly closely with our sense of identity. As we confuse our personal and professional identities, we deem any feedback, mistakes, or failures to be reflective of our inadequacies as a person.

In allowing this confusion to bleed into our perception of our identities and affect our sense of self-worth, we are unwittingly internalizing criticism so that it becomes toxic. Self-inflicted toxicity is a form of self-harm that happens when we let criticisms shape our self-worth rather than inform our growth. While constructive feedback should ideally guide us toward improvement, internalized negative thoughts amplify self-doubt, erode confidence, and become self-sabotaging rather than motivating.

Any individual who has dealt with imposter syndrome (every founder I've discussed this with) will recognize the symptoms of how unfairly we internalize criticism in negative ways.

In allowing ourselves to confuse and conflate our sense of self with our roles at work, we self-inflict criticism in a myriad of ways that can create a mental loop of harsh judgments that distort reality. In doing so, we focus solely on weaknesses without appreciating our strengths or progress. When unchecked, this pattern can damage both personal well-being and productivity, as it gradually shifts from helpful self-awareness to a destructive perfectionistic mindset. Recognizing and reframing these thoughts is the key to breaking the cycle of self-abuse. Allowing criticism to serve its purpose as a tool for growth rather than a weapon against oneself is essential to growth and success, both professionally and personally.

Ultimately, a strong organizational culture that values constructive criticism, encourages open communication, and actively supports inclusivity is a powerful foundation for long-term success. By fostering this type of culture, organizations not only enhance employee performance and retention but also create a legacy of growth, resilience, and innovation that can adapt to changing environments and diverse global perspectives.

A vibrant, adaptable culture is one where every voice matters, and values are lived daily, creating an environment where everyone can thrive.

Constructive Criticism and The Impact of Leadership

Criticism, when wielded thoughtfully, is one of the most transformative tools in an organization. It serves as a guiding force, illuminating paths for improvement and unlocking potential in individuals and teams. Yet, the true power of criticism lies not in the act itself but in how it is delivered and embraced. Constructive criticism—rooted in respect, empathy, and a focus on growth—can shape an organization's culture, strengthen relationships, and inspire remarkable achievements.

Have you ever dealt with a manager who gave feedback that was so vague it made fortune cookies seem specific?

or

Have you ever worked with a leader whose feedback made you feel like it was a pep talk from your most supportive friend?

At its core, constructive criticism provides clarity. It pinpoints areas for improvement while acknowledging strengths, creating a balanced framework for growth. Unlike toxic or poorly delivered feedback, which diminishes morale and undermines trust, constructive criticism uplifts. It shows individuals that their contributions are valued and that there is a belief in their ability to improve. In this way, criticism transforms from a dreaded experience into an opportunity for development.

A 2022 study by Harvard Business School analyzed the impact of constructive feedback on over 1,500 professionals across various industries. Participants receiving personalized, weekly constructive guidance showed a 9% increase in project delivery rates and a 12% improvement in output quality. This was largely due to heightened motivation and self-confidence, demonstrating how thoughtful feedback directly supports performance and morale.

Leaders play a pivotal role in setting the tone for how criticism is perceived and utilized within an organization. Effective leaders understand that criticism is not about fault-finding but about fostering progress. They approach feedback as an art form, using it to motivate and guide their teams. By delivering feedback with empathy and specificity, leaders create an environment where individuals feel supported in their efforts to grow.

Consider the difference between two leaders. One focuses solely on pointing out mistakes, leaving team members discouraged and uncertain about how to improve. The other takes the time to frame criticism constructively, highlighting successes while offering actionable steps for addressing challenges. The second leader not only empowers their team but also fosters a culture where feedback is welcomed as a tool for learning rather than feared as a source of shame.

To lead through constructive criticism effectively, leaders must model the behavior they wish to see. This means being open to feedback themselves, demonstrating vulnerability, and showing a willingness to grow. When leaders invite and act on feedback, they create a culture of mutual respect and continuous improvement. Employees are more likely to engage with feedback positively when they see their leaders doing the same.

Several psychological theories can help us understand how people respond to criticism. Maslow's treatise on the Hierarchy of Needs and Emotional Intelligence offers a critical perspective. Maslow's work is a theory of human motivation. Maslow proposed five levels of human needs and that individuals must satisfy their basic needs before moving on to higher-level needs. The five levels of needs are:

> - Physiological needs (e.g., food, water, shelter); Safety needs (e.g., security, stability, protection)
>
> - Love and belonging needs (e.g., intimacy, friendship, family) Esteem needs (e.g., self-respect, confidence, recognition)
>
> - Self-actualization needs (e.g., personal growth, fulfillment, meaning) When we receive criticism, it can threaten our self-esteem.

Criticism that is not constructive or positive can make us feel bad about ourselves and our abilities. Some people become so conditioned to "not good enough" that they struggle to accept positive feedback, always expecting something else. This inability to receive praise reflects a mental injury that has not been addressed, and as a manager, we need to create safe spaces for these individuals to accept compliments on their work. This ties into the concept of Emotional Intelligence, or the ability to understand and manage our own emotions as well as the emotions of others.

Empathy is a cornerstone of constructive criticism. Leaders who take the time to understand the emotions and perspectives of their team members can deliver feedback in a way that resonates and inspires. Empathy also helps leaders navigate the fine line between being direct and being supportive, ensuring that their message is both clear and encouraging.

Constructive criticism also requires a focus on solutions. Feedback that merely identifies problems without offering pathways for improvement can feel hollow and unhelpful. Leaders should provide specific, actionable advice that empowers individuals to address challenges and achieve their goals. By doing so, they transform criticism into a catalyst for growth.

The organizational benefits of constructive criticism are profound. Teams that embrace feedback as a learning tool are more innovative, resilient, and collaborative. They are unafraid to take risks, knowing that mistakes will be met with support rather than blame. This fosters an environment of trust and psychological safety, where creativity thrives, and performance soars.

Ultimately, the role of criticism in an organization is to build bridges—between individuals and their potential, between teams and their shared goals, and between leaders and their vision for success. Leaders who wield constructive criticism with empathy and purpose not only elevate their teams but also set the foundation for a culture of excellence and continuous improvement.

By redefining criticism as an opportunity for connection and growth, organizations can transform challenges into achievements, unlocking the full potential of their people and their purpose.

Constructive criticism is a catalyst for growth, guiding individuals and teams toward their highest potential with clarity and compassion. Effective leaders inspire growth by delivering feedback with empathy, transforming challenges into opportunities for learning and achievement.

Balancing a Culture of Constructive Criticism
Practical Steps for any Leader

Creating a thriving workplace hinges on fostering a feedback-rich culture, where constructive criticism and positive reinforcement work in harmony. When both elements are embraced, they fuel growth, innovation, and trust, creating an environment where employees feel valued and empowered.

The key is balance: while constructive criticism provides a roadmap for improvement, positive feedback acknowledges successes and reinforces confidence. Together, they form a powerful foundation for individual and collective excellence.

Have you ever been part of a team where mistakes weren't just tolerated, but recognized as stepping stones to greatness?

Constructive criticism, when delivered thoughtfully, sharpens skills and clarifies goals. It focuses on behaviors, not personal traits, ensuring feedback is actionable and respectful. This approach empowers individuals to understand their areas of improvement while preserving their dignity. It also cultivates a mindset where feedback is seen as an opportunity rather than a threat, fostering resilience and adaptability across the organization.

Positive reinforcement complements this by celebrating strengths and achievements. Recognizing effort and success builds trust, morale, and motivation. Employees who feel appreciated are more likely to take pride in their work and invest in their growth. Positive feedback is not merely about offering praise; it is about highlighting what works well, creating a sense of clarity and direction that encourages continued success.

A culture of feedback flourishes when these two elements—constructive criticism and positive reinforcement—are integrated seamlessly. For example, a leader might begin a feedback session by acknowledging an employee's recent achievements, creating an atmosphere of trust and appreciation. From there, they can introduce areas for improvement, framing challenges as opportunities to build on existing strengths. This balance not only helps employees accept feedback more openly but also fosters a sense of support and encouragement.

Organizations that value this dual approach recognize the importance of psychological safety. Employees need to feel secure in taking risks and making mistakes, knowing that their efforts will be met with understanding and guidance. This safety net encourages innovation, as individuals are more likely to experiment, learn, and grow when fear of criticism is replaced with constructive dialogue and genuine recognition.

Leaders play a pivotal role in modeling this culture. By demonstrating openness to feedback and regularly offering both constructive criticism and positive reinforcement, they set the tone for the organization. Their actions signal that feedback is a tool for growth, not a weapon of judgment. Leaders who actively seek input and acknowledge contributions create an environment where feedback flows freely and productively.

Consider a scenario where a team completes a challenging project. A leader who prioritizes positive reinforcement might highlight the team's perseverance and creativity in overcoming obstacles. At the same time, they could offer constructive insights on areas where processes could be refined for future success. This balanced approach not only reinforces the team's accomplishments but also encourages continuous improvement.

The benefits of a feedback-rich culture extend beyond individual development. Teams that embrace feedback as a collective practice become more collaborative and innovative. They are equipped to navigate challenges with a shared sense of purpose, leveraging their combined strengths to achieve ambitious goals. Moreover, organizations that invest in this culture see tangible results in engagement, retention, and overall performance.

If you want to improve your skills, keep the following guidelines for improving yourself, your leadership, and your team:

- Constructive feedback fosters a growth mindset. When criticism focuses on behaviors, not people, employees are empowered to take risks and evolve.

- Connect work to meaning beyond profits. Purpose-driven teams withstand external skepticism and channel dissent into innovation.

- Lead with vulnerability and empathy. Modeling openness builds bonds, enabling groups to leverage setbacks for growth.

- Let go to motivate. Grant teams with autonomy on implementation after articulating an inspiring vision and watch as discretionary effort multiplies.

- Engineer feedback systems that reinforce organizational values. Publicly praised ideals sustain engagement over time.

- Address ineffective communication styles promptly. Toxic patterns demoralize quickly if left unresolved, spreading dysfunction.

- Celebrate even the smallest of collective wins with sincerity. Recognizing incremental progress gives confidence for bolder aspirations.

- Diagnose cultural blind spots that skew perception. Seek input from across the entire hierarchy, which will broaden understanding of challenges and help managers adapt strategies.

- Skillfully leveraging workplace feedback for learning will unlock potential.

Over time, leaders gain more ingenuity and dedication by upholding dignity while pushing teams to grow.

Positive feedback and constructive criticism are not opposing forces; they are complementary tools that, when used effectively, unlock potential and drive progress. By fostering a culture that values both, organizations can create workplaces where every individual feels supported, motivated, and inspired to reach their full potential.

In the end, the balance between recognizing success and addressing opportunities for growth lies at the heart of a thriving organization. It's a delicate yet rewarding dynamic that builds trust, fuels innovation, and ensures that both individuals and teams are positioned to excel.

By embracing feedback we celebrate the strengths and successes that build confidence and become a tool for continuous improvement. In doing so, we create workplaces where innovation, resilience, and collaboration flourish.

Choose Wisely

Evaluating Corporate Culture and Constructive Feedback
During Job Interviews

Imagine you're Indiana Jones, choosing the right chalice. In this case, the right choice will bring you growth and joy at work. Choosing unwisely will place you in a toxic environment that stifles your growth and breeds self-doubt.

Have you ever had a job interview where the conversation was so open and engaging that you could already see yourself thriving in a culture of mutual respect, shared learning, and growth-focused feedback?

Interviewing for a new role is as much about your opportunity to assess the organization as it is about showcasing your own skills.

Corporate culture and the way feedback is delivered are critical factors in determining whether you will thrive in a new environment. The interview process offers subtle yet telling clues about whether the company's culture aligns with your values and whether the team, including your prospective boss, values constructive criticism as a tool for growth.

As you engage in conversations during the interview process, you should spend some time focusing on the atmosphere created by your interactions. Begin by observing the tone of communication. A company that prioritizes constructive feedback is likely to foster a sense of curiosity, openness, and respect. Pay attention to how your interviewer responds to your questions and ideas. Are they listening attentively and showing genuine interest, or do they seem dismissive or hurried? The way people interact with you in the interview often mirrors their day-to-day behavior.

One effective approach is to ask thoughtful questions about the company's culture and leadership style. Instead of directly asking about feedback practices, try exploring how the organization values development and learning. You might ask your prospective manager to share an example of a time when they provided feedback that helped an employee improve, or how the company manages people who are struggling. The way they recount this experience can reveal a lot. If their story highlights encouragement, collaboration, and actionable advice, you're likely in the company of a leader who embraces constructive criticism. Conversely, if their response focuses on pointing out mistakes without offering solutions, it may suggest a less supportive approach to growth.

Another revealing angle is to inquire about how the team celebrates successes and learns from challenges. A culture that values constructive criticism will view mistakes as opportunities to learn rather than failures to avoid. Listen carefully to how they describe their processes for addressing setbacks. Are there mentions of support, innovation, and a focus on progress? Or does the narrative lean toward blame and defensiveness? The language they use will offer insights into whether the team cultivates resilience and continuous improvement.

Make sure you ask questions about company activities and pay attention to the stories interviewers share about their colleagues and workplace dynamics. If you hear about collaboration, shared learning, and mutual respect, these are positive signs. On the other hand, anecdotes about cutthroat competition or individuals being singled out for errors might indicate a culture where feedback is more punitive than constructive.

The way the interviewers speak about each other also matters. Do they express appreciation for their colleagues' contributions, or do their remarks carry an undertone of criticism?

During your visit, observe non-verbal cues and subtle details about the work environment. Is the office atmosphere warm and inviting, or does it feel tense and overly formal? Small things, like how people greet one another or how they interact in shared spaces, can provide clues about the organization's values. Constructive cultures are often marked by friendly exchanges and an overall sense of psychological safety.

Ask about professional development opportunities, as they often reflect the company's approach to growth. Companies that prioritize constructive feedback tend to invest in training programs, mentorship, and coaching. If the interviewers enthusiastically discuss such initiatives, it's a strong indication that the organization values personal and professional growth. On the other hand, if development is treated as an afterthought, it could suggest a lack of commitment to fostering a supportive culture.

Finally, consider your own feelings throughout the process. Did you feel heard, respected, and valued during the interview? The best interviews are not interrogations but collaborative conversations where both parties feel empowered. If you leave feeling inspired and energized, it's a strong sign that the culture might be a good fit for you. Trust your instincts. Sometimes, the way a place makes you feel can be the clearest indicator of whether it aligns with your values.

By staying attentive to these nuances, you can gain a clearer understanding of the company's culture and whether it is a place where you can thrive. After all, joining a new team is not just about finding a job—it's about finding an environment where you can grow, contribute, and succeed together.

Finding the right fit means seeking a culture where respect, feedback, and shared values align with your aspirations for growth and success.

The Value of Rewarding Mistakes

Mistakes are not only inevitable, they are also essential for growth and the creation of a positive corporate culture. Take a moment to consider the oxymoron inherent in this statement: Errors are required to create positive results.

The "fail fast" approach, widely adopted in tech and other agile industries, advocates for rapid experimentation and quick learning from mistakes. It empowers teams to take calculated risks and correct missteps early, minimizing risks while maximizing opportunities for growth and innovation.

When the "fail fast" approach is combined with the concept of "positive mistakes," a robust framework for constructive feedback and improvement is created.

Have you ever been part of a team where owning mistakes was applauded?

"Positive mistakes" are errors or missteps that provide valuable insights, fostering learning, growth, and innovation. These types of mistakes, often called "learning opportunities," encourage individuals and teams to explore new solutions, refine skills, and deepen their understanding. They differ from avoidable or negligent mistakes in that they occur within a framework of intentional effort and curiosity rather than carelessness or lack of preparation.

For an approach that combines failing fast and positive mistakes to succeed, an organizational culture that embraces both mistakes and failure is essential.

Building a culture that views mistakes as progress requires a foundation of psychological safety, where employees feel comfortable experimenting without fear of reprimand. Leaders play a critical role in cultivating this environment, normalizing the idea that mistakes are integral to learning and improvement.

By sharing their mistakes openly and discussing the lessons they learned, leaders demonstrate that errors are not setbacks but steps forward. This approach encourages employees to stretch beyond their comfort zones, make bold decisions, and pursue innovative ideas with confidence, knowing that their contributions—successes and failures alike—are valued. Over time, a team that feels safe to take risks develops resilience and agility, becoming better equipped to handle future challenges and increasingly able to drive meaningful progress.

Positive mistakes occur when employees attempt new approaches, challenge existing norms, or take on ambitious tasks, gaining insights into themselves, even if the immediate outcome falls short.

Mistakes like these can be great opportunities to identify areas where we can improve our processes, discover potential weaknesses in our systems, and develop valuable skills that contribute to our overall growth.

For example, when a team starts using a new project management tool, they might face some challenges at first. But through those early hiccups, they learn to refine their approach and discover new ways to enhance collaboration that benefit everyone in the organization. Similarly, when marketing teams try out unconventional strategies, even if they don't always succeed, they often gain useful insights that sharpen their future campaigns.

The fail-fast mindset complements positive mistakes by encouraging rapid iteration, constant feedback, and timely course corrections. Instead of fixating only on revenue or traditional metrics, organizations that embrace this approach often set clear learning goals for each experiment. This empowers teams to assess their progress through the valuable insights gained and the adjustments made along the way, recognizing that every setback is actually a stepping-stone towards finding the right solution.

Making positive mistakes and failing quickly must be accepted as ongoing processes, not just one-time events. Teams should reflect on what was effective, what wasn't, and the reasons behind these outcomes. To make the learning process effective, teams must conduct regular reviews of lessons learned, ensuring that valuable insights are retained. If they fail to do so, they risk repeating past mistakes. Ignoring or stubbornly repeating these errors is unproductive and undesirable.

A culture centered on learning encourages staff to take risks and learn from mistakes, promoting creativity and innovation by creating a judgment-free environment for exploring unconventional ideas and testing new solutions. When team members feel their contributions are appreciated, they become more engaged in their work, which boosts morale. As time progresses, employees and teams develop greater resilience, enhanced skills, and improved capabilities to tackle challenges innovatively, viewing obstacles as opportunities to apply lessons learned and experiment with new strategies.

Documenting and periodically reviewing mistakes helps teams track common challenges and pinpoint the areas that need additional training or resources. Equally importantly, by documenting and creating case studies on the learning, we can share these insights across the organization, enabling a culture of continuous learning and process refinement.

Leaders who value learning as much as results are those who create the work environments that support continuous improvement. Teams who feel valued, confident, and motivated by leaders who encourage learning from mistakes are far more resilient and productive, especially during times of uncertainty. This resilience translates into tangible business benefits as teams move faster, adapt to changing market demands, and innovate with confidence.

When we quickly recognize and analyze our mistakes, they don't feel like failures but rather signposts on our journey of progress. By embracing a fail-fast, learn-faster culture, companies gain the flexibility to iterate, innovate, and keep improving, transforming each setback into a valuable stepping-stone toward success.

Such an approach is not merely a trend, it is a transformative way to empower people, grow the business, and position the organization as a learning-focused, adaptive, and forward-thinking entity.

When we view mistakes as opportunities for learning and innovation, we create a culture where growth is not only possible but inevitable.

Ego and Self-Esteem at Work

While constructive criticism builds support, poorly delivered criticism and feedback deflates and destroys an organization's culture. Not only do ill-chosen words deflate confidence, but the uncertainty created from a single instance of poorly delivered feedback can do more damage to people's self-esteem than managers can ever hope to build through months of effort.

Self-esteem is critical to success and affects an individual's overall perception of self-worth and competence. It shapes how we interpret situations, approach challenges, and envision possibilities for ourselves.

Have you ever worked with someone whose confidence was so contagious that everyone around them was lifted to new heights?

Constructive criticism plays a crucial role in our growth, but it's important to deliver feedback in a thoughtful way. When feedback comes across as harsh, it can really shake an employee's confidence and negatively impact our workplace culture. Just one moment of serious criticism can overshadow all the encouragement given over months, leading employees to struggle with self-doubt that can hurt their self-esteem.

Self-esteem is integral to anyone's success, influencing how we interpret situations, approach challenges, and envision our potential. Unfortunately, people who struggle with self-doubt and self-worth issues often misinterpret those with balanced self-esteem as being egotistical. Projecting their anxieties onto others, they attack the more well balanced individuals as a fear response, much as a cornered animal would.

These responses often arise from projection—a psychological mechanism where individuals impose their insecurities, fears, or flaws onto others. When someone with low self-worth meets a confident person, they might misinterpret that confidence as arrogance, as it starkly contrasts with their self-image. Instead of recognizing this confidence as healthy self-esteem, they project their insecurities onto the other individual and view their balanced confidence as excessive or even intimidating. Unfortunately, this projection leads them to miss valuable opportunities for growth and re-evaluation.

This behavioral tendency can also be reinforced by a fear of comparison. When someone with low self-esteem sees another individual confidently expressing their abilities or ideas, they question the value of their own contributions, and doing so triggers feelings of inadequacy or jealousy, intensifying their discomfort. To cope, they might label the other person as egotistical or self-centered, which serves as a way to diminish the perceived threat.

By casting a confident person in a negative light to themselves and others, an individual is seeking to avoid confronting their own self-doubts and instead shift the focus outward, positioning the confident individual as the problem rather than examining their own insecurities.

People with low self-esteem are often overly critical of themselves, and may assume others judge them just as harshly. Therefore, when they see someone openly demonstrating confidence, they might believe that person is judging or looking down on them, even if this isn't the case. This can fuel resentment and prompt them to label the person as egotistical to defend against feelings of vulnerability.

In essence, individuals struggling with self-worth issues often misinterpret confidence as arrogance because they are unsure of the difference between self-esteem and ego.

To those lacking self-assurance, authentic confidence can feel threatening or even antagonistic, prompting defensive responses. This reaction can create misunderstandings, as the confident person's balanced self-esteem is mistaken for something it's not. By understanding these dynamics, both parties can navigate interactions more compassionately, recognizing that confidence isn't arrogance, it's simply a reflection of self-acceptance.

This brings us to a key point: Self-esteem and ego are often confused, yet they fundamentally differ in how they shape an individual's perception of self-worth and interactions with others. While self-esteem is grounded in a realistic and balanced sense of one's intrinsic value, ego tends to be more reactive, shaped by external comparisons, and often requires constant validation from others. This need for external validation reflect internal insecurities that they seek to mask through an air of confidence and superiority.

Self-esteem represents an inner sense of worth that isn't easily swayed by external opinions or achievements. People with high self-esteem understand their strengths and weaknesses, and this awareness gives them a stable foundation. Because their self-worth is intrinsic, they don't feel threatened by constructive feedback or the success of others.

Attempts to accomplish are valued, not just successes, as they tend to view challenges as opportunities for growth, secure in their capacity to improve. This internal stability encourages them to engage openly, take creative risks, and collaborate without fear of inadequacy or competition. Self-esteem, therefore, serves as a bedrock for resilience, openness, and empathy in personal and professional relationships.

In contrast, ego is often driven by external validation and comparison. Rather than being based on one's internal sense of value, ego tends to inflate or deflate based on external circumstances and feedback. A person with a strong ego may find it difficult to handle criticism or failure because their self-worth is conditional on maintaining a certain image or level of superiority.

Ego-driven individuals often feel a need to prove themselves, even at the expense of others or of their own long-term growth.

When faced with feedback, ego-driven individuals often respond defensively, perceiving it as a personal attack rather than a chance to improve. Their ego can thus create barriers to genuine connection, collaboration, and self-improvement because it is more invested in protecting an image than in personal development.

While self-esteem promotes growth and connection, ego often builds walls, as it thrives on being "better than" others. In contrast, when individuals act from self-esteem, they are more likely to engage authentically and constructively, creating positive environments and relationships.

When actions stem from ego, individuals often become competitive, and seek to mask their insecurities, which often leads to conflicts and missed opportunities for learning. This leads to a form of toxicity where the ego-driven individuals seek to exclude others due to their hidden insecurities, rather than embrace others who might expose their frailties.

When I hire teams to work with me, I always explain that I focus on hiring people from whom I can learn and who share a learning mindset. I do so because I recognize that there are always people better than I am, and I do not feel threatened by anyone else's superior competence in any area. In fact, I embrace the skills, wisdom, and intelligence of my team as my opportunities to learn from them! I expect them to do the same, and together, every team member will grow each other's potential.

In contrast, leaders motivated by ego face challenges with this approach because they think their significance relies on being the most skilled, knowledgeable, or authoritative individual present.

Consequently, they may prefer to hire individuals who enhance their sense of superiority instead of those who challenge or excel beyond them.

When a leader hires people who bring strengths to the areas where they may lack expertise, teams become more well-rounded, innovative, and capable of tackling complex challenges. Such leaders are confident enough to admit what they don't know and prioritize the organization's success over personal recognition. Their sense of self-worth isn't contingent on being the best at everything but rather on contributing to an effective, high-performing team.

While I am by no means perfect, I always explain to the teams I work with that my job is to ensure that everyone around me has the tools they need to succeed. Therefore, I work for them. If I am successful in providing them with those tools, the organization is well prepared to succeed.

This self-aware approach creates a culture of mutual respect and trust, where team members feel empowered to share their expertise without fear of outshining the leader. It fosters an environment in which ideas can be challenged, creativity can thrive, and innovation is encouraged, as everyone understands that their strengths are viewed as assets rather than threats. Leaders who embrace this philosophy cultivate teams that are adaptable and resilient, as they encourage continuous learning and growth across the organization.

Ego, on the other hand, can lead to disastrous hiring decisions, as an ego-driven leader often shies away from hiring individuals who could bring skills that surpass their own, fearing they might diminish their perceived authority. This fear limits the potential of both the team and the organization, as it discourages the diversity of thought, skill, and perspective that drives real progress.

In essence, the philosophy of hiring people who are better than yourself is an act of humility and self-assurance. It reflects a leader's belief that the best outcomes come from collaboration and diverse strengths.

Ultimately, self-esteem is a quiet confidence that doesn't require others to diminish for one to feel strong, while ego seeks validation and dominance, often at the expense of personal and interpersonal growth. Nurturing self-esteem rather than ego enables individuals and teams to focus on shared goals, learn from failures, and contribute positively to collective success.

Balanced self-esteem fuels personal and professional success, allowing us to connect with others authentically and build stronger teams.

Criticism's Impact on Self-Esteem

Leadership isn't about being the most skilled or knowledgeable but about empowering those around you, leveraging their expertise to achieve a shared vision.

People with a strong sense of self-esteem engage fully, take constructive risks, and view setbacks as growth opportunities. In contrast, those with low self-esteem avoid risks, struggle with change, and are sensitive to criticism. They often adopt a fixed mindset that can be difficult to reverse.

Have you ever received feedback so thoughtful that it made you realize just how much potential you really have?

I hope you have! Unfortunately, even the hardiest of characters will be negatively impacted by poorly delivered feedback. Worse, negative feedback is more commonly delivered.

To fully appreciate the psychological impact of criticism, we must examine how harsh or unconstructive feedback can harm self-esteem, cause stress, and result in disengagement.

No matter the context in which it is delivered, poorly delivered feedback will create uncertainty and stress. When disengagement occurs as a result, many managers treat these behavioral responses as isolated issues and choose the most expedient path to managing a problem rather than the best long-term strategy.

If you have ever been in a similar situation, ask yourself: Why are you there if you have no value? Because you do have value. Your boss' lack of proper self-esteem is the issue.

Unfortunately, many workplace cultures erode rather than empower employee self-esteem. In these organizations, management practices prioritize compliance over empowerment and rely on criticism as a pressure-based motivational tool. The negative feedback used to push performance focuses on 'tried-and-true methods' and diminishes individual confidence, fostering an environment where employees inevitably feel they fall short in the eyes of management, initiating a downward spiral of self-doubt and disengagement.

Employees who facing constant negativity. Unfortunately, because success is not obtainable, the ongoing negative feedback will cement itself in their self-perceptions and transform into self-loathing, annihilating the foundation of self-esteem employees typically build over a lifetime.

Employees who receive feedback without constructive suggestions for improvement will often rationalize that they must work harder to improve their flaws. But when success remains elusive, they will internalize the feedback as a reflection of their core abilities and disengage. The resulting self-criticism can evolve into self-loathing, eroding the self-esteem that has likely been a lifelong foundation.

Instead of contributing positively, these individuals begin to view themselves as less capable, creative, or valuable than their peers, limiting their ability to make a positive impact.

Today's mental health crisis poses a significant threat to organizational resilience and sustainability, and leaders can no longer afford to ignore its effects on the workplace. Studies show that cultures rooted in criticism rather than empowerment lead to declines in performance, collaboration, and innovation. When employees internalize negative feedback, their motivation and willingness to take risks diminish, leading them to protect themselves by reducing effort, avoiding teamwork, and missing advancement opportunities. This withdrawal not only lowers productivity but can also result in anxiety, depression, and trauma from chronic workplace stress.

The damage goes beyond individuals, affecting teams and overall workplace culture. When criticism becomes habitual, trust erodes, burnout increases, and self-preservation takes precedence over collaboration. In these conditions, employees often avoid conflict, fearing it may provoke more criticism. This tendency to retreat prevents effective conflict resolution and allows tensions to fester, spreading toxicity throughout teams and the organization.

Some leaders worry that restoring self-esteem could undermine accountability, but research shows otherwise. Companies with strengths-based feedback, psychologically safe environments, and mental health support excel in profitability, innovation, and retention. Workers respond positively when treated with respect, reciprocating organizational care with greater engagement and discretionary effort. Building this trust requires a shift from outdated, critical management practices to an approach that truly values employees.

The opportunity for positive change is within reach for leaders willing to challenge traditional norms. By supporting self-esteem, leaders create environments where employees can handle conflict constructively and with resilience. Coaching and peer support help individuals reframe conflicts as growth opportunities, fostering open communication and trust. Confident employees feel safer addressing concerns directly, knowing leaders will approach conflicts with understanding, not judgment.

A healthy self-image supports not only conflict management but also mental well-being. Employees with low self-esteem may interpret even constructive feedback negatively, feeding a self-destructive cycle that exacerbates anxiety and self-doubt. Conversely, a stable self-image acts as a psychological buffer, enabling employees to process criticism in context and maintain optimism. Tragically, many employees struggling with mental health challenges fear that seeking support at work could harm their reputation. They worry that disclosing issues may lead to unfair judgments or stigma among peers, leaving them isolated and struggling in silence.

Organizations that prioritize mental health create spaces where employees feel safe seeking support. Leaders can foster openness by sharing their mental health journeys, promoting suicide prevention training, highlighting counseling services, and providing mental health days. This transparency communicates that speaking up is not a weakness but a sign of self-awareness. When employees trust they can openly discuss challenges, they're able to contribute fully and authentically.

Creating a culture of trust and compassion requires vulnerability and humility from leaders. By modeling openness about their own challenges, leaders encourage reciprocal openness, building a foundation for mutual trust. Employees who believe their challenges will be met with empathy unlock new levels of creativity and commitment. As Brené Brown explains, "having the courage to be vulnerable is about showing up when you can't predict or control the outcome." Leaders who embrace this mindset foster an environment where employees feel empowered to take risks, learn from challenges, and drive the organization forward.

Thoughtful feedback strengthens confidence and inspires growth, helping individuals see their potential and pursue it with determination.

Self-Defeat Through Non-Constructive Criticism

When the Hunter believes they are the Farmer, everyone fails,
because the Hunter only knows how to harvest

It is only through learning from our mistakes that anyone can become great.

Have you ever helped someone turn tough feedback into a motivational mantra
that help spark their growth?

Many people's journey passes through defeat. Some learn from their missteps, while others, in their attempt to shirk responsibility, blame others for any misfortune. Like gardeners who dream only of a bountiful harvest, they do not understand how to grow their crops effectively. So, when faced with adverse conditions, they make choices that inflict rather than mitigate damage to their crops. When their actions results in weaker harvests, they cast the blame on others, seeking to avoid responsibility for their mistakes.

When we learn to accept that mistakes are steps toward success, we can shift our focus from a punitive management style to a growth-oriented mindset and adopt a supportive feedback style.

Every business owner aspires to achieve peak performance, though how they define it can vary widely. Some may build a lifestyle business that provides a comfortable living for their family, while others might aim to make a global impact. Regardless of the scale or purpose, success comes down to setting and managing expectations—both for oneself and for the team. When expectations are unclear, misunderstandings arise, leading to inevitable disappointment and, often, a toxic work environment.

One of the primary causes of toxicity in organizations is top-down management that fails to value employees' input. Leaders who act as though employees work for them miss a fundamental truth: in effective organizations, leaders work *for* their employees. The goal of a leader is to empower their team with the resources, support, and direction they need to succeed. When employees feel valued, they contribute more meaningfully to the organization's growth.

Yet, some leaders adopt an authoritarian mindset, believing their perspective is the only one that matters. This narrow view breeds a culture of criticism that is not constructive and can quickly become toxic. Criticism, when delivered without respect or guidance, demoralizes employees, diminishes productivity, and ultimately harms the organization. Constructive feedback, by contrast, is essential for growth. It provides actionable guidance and encourages improvement, motivating employees to continue striving toward excellence.

Consider three examples of feedback on a project briefing note:

- "This is a good start! If you could add specifics about the time and costs required, that would be very helpful. Do you have everything you need to do so?"

- "This draft is not good enough. It's lacking too many details to be useful; keep working on it."

- "Why do you always send me incomplete drafts? If you needed more time, you should have told me instead of sending this."

The first response encourages improvement with specific, constructive feedback. It respects the effort put into the draft while guiding the next steps. This approach aligns with effective leadership practices, creating a culture of growth and support. The second statement, while direct, lacks actionable guidance, making it difficult for the employee to know how to improve. The third statement attacks the individual rather than addressing the work, which can lead to defensiveness and disengagement.

When leaders shape their feedback with the team's growth in mind, they help establish a culture where criticism is constructive rather than damaging. Toxic criticism, however, is not actionable. It often targets the individual rather than their work, eroding confidence, morale, and trust within teams. If unaddressed, such criticism can spiral into chronic issues, affecting employees' mental health, productivity, and ultimately, the organization's success.

The consequences of toxic criticism are severe. Employees subjected to it often feel undervalued, leading to low job satisfaction and decreased motivation. In toxic environments, stress levels rise, as employees operate in constant fear of negative feedback. Chronic stress has well-documented effects on physical and mental health, impacting everything from productivity to team morale. In time, this environment fosters disengagement, withdrawal from team activities, and resistance to taking risks or speaking up.

High turnover is another common outcome of a toxic culture. As employees seek healthier work environments, the organization faces increased recruitment costs and a potential decline in reputation. Replacing an employee is estimated to cost up to 220% of their salary, a significant expense exacerbated by a tarnished reputation, which can deter top talent from joining. If left unchecked, a culture of toxic criticism not only harms the immediate team but can also negatively impact client relationships, public perception, and strategic growth.

Effective leaders recognize that while criticism is necessary, it must be constructive and respectful. This approach supports the well-being of employees and strengthens the organization's foundations. When employees feel valued and supported, they are more likely to be motivated, innovative, and engaged, creating a positive cycle of growth and success.

Addressing toxic behaviors involves setting clear expectations for constructive feedback and investing in policies and training that foster respectful communication. Leaders must model the behavior they wish to see, demonstrating a commitment to a culture that prioritizes respect, support, and growth.

Quickly and effectively tackling toxicity is essential not only for enhancing individual experiences but also for the overall health and success of the organization. This involves putting in place policies and training that promote positive feedback and communication, while also ensuring that leaders and managers are prepared to recognize and confront toxic behaviors. Such an effort necessitates commitment from the highest levels of the organization to transform the culture, establishing an environment of respect, support, and constructive interaction and feedback.

The long-term consequences of a culture that tolerates or promotes toxic criticism are severe, and they affect the organization's overall effectiveness and success.

Addressing and transforming any forms of toxicity is essential for creating a workplace where employees feel valued and supported. Doing so will only lead to a more productive, innovative, and successful organization.

An organizational transformation from toxic to constructive is not easy, as inertia and complacency struggle against any change. But the alternative, allowing a toxic culture to exist, is far more damaging. Tolerating toxicity is the equivalent of committing organizational suicide.

Leaders who foster and encourage constructive feedback create an atmosphere where employees can flourish, leading to a healthier and more productive workplace organization.

Essentially, changing criticism from a negative influence to a positive one is a key investment in the organization's future. Fostering a feedback culture that emphasizes growth rather than judgment creates a workplace where employees feel appreciated and inspired. In this type of environment, innovation thrives, collaboration strengthens, and the organization as a whole is better prepared to reach its strategic objectives.

By identifying and mitigating the sources of toxic criticism, leaders are taking concrete action to improve the well-being of their employees and enhance the overall performance and success of their teams and organizations.

Choosing words that uplift rather than tear down creates a ripple effect of resilience and optimism in every workplace interaction.

Self-Loathing and Its Impact on Management and Team Dynamics

Self-loathing is a complex psychological experience that profoundly affects the way individuals engage with themselves and those around them. In a workplace setting, this mindset often manifests itself as perfectionism, risk aversion, emotional volatility, and an underlying fear of inadequacy.

For individuals in management, recognizing how self-loathing affects team dynamics is essential, as its influence reaches beyond the individual, affecting morale, productivity, and workplace culture. Managers who spot self-loathing behaviors and implement supportive strategies can cultivate an environment that encourages growth, strengthens resilience, and promotes a culture of positivity empathy. These managers are leaders!

> *Have you ever cheered on a peer and helped them transform their inner critic into their biggest cheerleader?*

Self-loathing affects people's relationships with friends, colleagues, and managers. Individuals with self-loathing tendencies will often impose impossibly high standards on themselves, viewing any mistakes as proof of their inadequacy.

Often, perfectionist tendencies are viewed as a high level of diligence. However, in many individuals, perfectionism is indicative of anxiety. When faced with perfectionist behavior, a manager is well-placed to consider if the anxiety and unfair self-criticism are rooted in self-loathing. This analysis is warranted both to assist the individual and to preclude their tendencies from becoming toxic and negatively impacting those around them.

The unfair self-criticism that a perfectionist individual can inflict upon themselves often leads to emotional volatility, strained relationships, and a general stunting of emotional and professional connections. Within a team, this behavior contributes to increased tension, and colleagues often feel pressured to match unrealistic standards or avoid engagement.

When this occurs, rather than work to improve the situation, the individual who suffers from self-loathing begins to see their work and personal relationships as toxic. This is a defensive response they use to protect themselves from hurt. Sadly, they use these narratives to re-confirm their biases and justify their challenges as organizational toxicity and not reflective of their internal conflicts.

Leaving a job because of a toxic environment can signify a necessary escape from a harmful situation. However, if you consistently cite workplace toxicity as the reason for changing jobs, it might be time to reflect on whether the workplace is truly to blame.

This assessment will be scary to those afflicted. But we can only overcome our challenges by confronting ourselves truthfully. By honestly assessing whether you suffer from anxiety as a result of self-loathing, you are helping yourself overcome any internal challenges that reduce the satisfaction you receive at work and at home.

Managers who identify these patterns among colleagues and staff can help them address their challenges and lessen the effects on others by promoting healthier boundaries and encouraging more productive interactions. This begins with embracing self-compassion and modeling the desired behaviors for their colleagues and staff.

When leaders actively foster self-compassion, they contribute to a work environment where employees feel secure in their imperfections, allowing for learning and growth. By demonstrating a growth-focused attitude toward mistakes, leaders can inspire employees to confront self-critical thoughts, viewing errors as essential and natural components of their learning journeys.

Leaders who candidly share their mistakes and the lessons learned create a strong example by normalizing the belief that growth frequently arises from trial and error. This practice encourages everyone to view mistakes positively and lessens the pressure on team members to seem perfect. Over time, this decrease in pressure can empower even the most reserved individuals to overcome the cycle of self-criticism fueled by perceived failures.

> *In both our professional and personal lives, we must encourage people to accept that success requires failure first!*

Here's a relatable perspective: Wayne Gretzky scored on just 17.6% of his shots, indicating that 82.4% of the time he failed. Despite this clear shortcoming, he is regarded as one of the greatest hockey players of all time!

If Wayne Gretzky experienced failure 80% of the time, should you permit yourself to make mistakes sometimes? Please answer the question honestly and without qualifiers.

The answer, of course, is yes. Furthermore, if you don't make mistakes, it means you're either not trying to grow or you're refusing to allow yourself the opportunity to learn!

Leaders should motivate everyone to take chances, accept failures, and celebrate both big and small achievements. The distinction between big and small is a vital aspect that often goes unnoticed. A missed attempt can always lead to success. The more attempts you make, the better you adapt, learn, and grow. This is a success because it provides a chance to learn and enhance your skills. Ultimately, you must embrace mistakes, learn from them, and move forward grow.

Management can use constructive criticism and feedback to turn mistakes into a tool for combating self-loathing. However, for those grappling with negative self-images, feedback may be viewed as validation of their deepest insecurities. This creates a considerable challenge for the individuals involved as well as their coworkers and supervisors. The initial step in addressing this issue is to confront it directly, acknowledge its presence, and accept the discomfort that comes with overcoming it

Addressing this challenge can be tough. When we observe challenging behavior in others, we often see it as a singular moment. While it's important not to excuse poor actions, it is vital to reflect on the reasons behind their reactions. For individuals grappling with low self-esteem and self-hatred, these issues often stem from abusive experiences in their early years.

A child repeatedly told they are unworthy learns to feel worthless. When they face criticism, their inner dialogue echoes the harsh words of their oppressor. Initially, they develop defense mechanisms, anticipating that any errors will lead to attacks on their abilities, prompting them to construct barriers for protection.

This is beyond unfortunate because while they believe they are keeping pain out, these walls internalize, reinforce, and amplify the self-inflicted damage.

A child who experiences mental abuse and is repeatedly told they are fat, lazy, and stupid may start to believe these hurtful words. Even when they later realize these statements aren't true, their inner voice can still echo these negative messages when they make a mistake, leading them to feel that it was expected because of those unkind labels. This internal struggle can be very challenging. However, by confronting and challenging these harmful beliefs, we can help ourselves and others begin to see the source of this negativity for what it truly is.

Permission is a term that is often misunderstood. To overcome the self-inflicted torment people are burdened with as a result of abuse, individuals must recognize its cause and grant themselves permission to challenge false beliefs. They need to understand that the inner critic is unfairly skewing their viewpoint and ultimately allow themselves to accept that they are good, capable, valuable, and valued.

We need to learn how to tell that voice to fuck off.

It's a difficult battle, but by adopting constructive and fair feedback, managers can foster a supportive atmosphere that encourages individuals to confront and overcome their self-criticisms. As trust grows and misconceptions are addressed, people start to view feedback not as a judgement of their value but as a tool for achieving their potential and goals.

Setting healthy boundaries is crucial for combating self-loathing. Individuals facing this mindset often overwork themselves, seeking to validate their worth. Managers who demonstrate healthy boundaries—by limiting after-hours communication, promoting regular breaks, and taking personal time—emphasize that rest and balance are both valuable and essential

Entrepreneurs are frequently criticized for inadequate boundaries, merging work with personal life. Their dedication to their businesses is intertwined with their identity, which doesn't necessarily indicate self-loathing. Yet, entrepreneurs are often reluctant to disconnect, favoring multiple short breaks instead of longer vacations. A significant distinction lies in how they treat others; if they prioritize their employees' well-being, it suggests they likely maintain a healthier balance in their professional lives.

When employees observe their leaders valuing well-being, they are more inclined to perceive self-care as an essential component of their work life. This perspective counters the belief that unyielding productivity equates to commitment, aiding employees who struggle with self-worth to understand that their value is not exclusively linked to their output.

Celebrating successes is another powerful method for addressing self-loathing. Individuals who face challenges with self-worth often find it hard to acknowledge and celebrate their successes openly. It's much simpler to minimize achievements, as this tends to draw less attention.

Management can address this by creating regular opportunities to recognize both individual and team accomplishments. This can be done through public acknowledgments in meetings or personalized messages that emphasize contributions and celebrate wins. Genuine recognition for efforts helps employees link their work to positive results. Additionally, this practice enables individuals to subtly transform their self-view over time, perceiving their achievements as a true reflection of their skills rather than attributing them to external factors such as luck.

Providing access to mental health resources is essential for organizations dedicated to assisting those dealing with a variety of challenges, not just self-loathing. The underlying issues often stem from deep-rooted psychological difficulties that can only be addressed with professional support.

By providing resources such as counseling services, wellness initiatives, and mental health workshops, organizations show their commitment to overall well-being. Accessing these resources not only helps employees manage their mental health but also underscores that the organization values them beyond their output. This emphasis also fosters a trustful environment, allowing individuals to seek necessary assistance without fear of judgment, stigmatization, or repercussions.

Managers can also foster a culture of mentorship and peer support to help employees navigate self-loathing. Mentorship provides employees with a trusted advisor who offers guidance, encouragement, and constructive feedback in a safe, supportive context. Through mentorship, individuals struggling with self-doubt can gain perspective and learn to recognize their strengths. Additionally, peer support networks within the organization offer spaces for employees to share experiences, learn from each other, and feel understood. When employees feel connected to their colleagues and have access to mentors who believe in their potential, they are better equipped to counter the narrative of inadequacy that often accompanies self-loathing.

Ultimately, addressing self-loathing within a workplace context requires empathy, understanding, and a proactive approach. Management's role is to cultivate an environment that nurtures self-worth, supports balanced work habits, and champions growth. By creating a culture that values compassion, constructive feedback, and resilience, leaders can help team members move beyond self-loathing and embrace their potential. When employees feel valued and empowered, they bring their best selves to the organization, fostering a workplace culture that thrives on collaboration, trust, and mutual respect.

When we address our own insecurities, we free ourselves to lead with clarity and inspire others to rise to their fullest potential.

Developing Resilience to Criticism

Criticism is an inevitable part of professional life. While we have established that constructive feedback can inspire growth, it often stirs discomfort, particularly for those who may take criticism personally or feel vulnerable to its impact.

Building resilience in response to criticism doesn't mean dismissing or ignoring feedback. On the contrary, it involves self-regulation, constructive engagement with feedback, and management of the accompanying stress. Techniques that foster resilience, such as mindfulness, reframing negative thoughts, and developing emotional intelligence, are essential to transforming criticism from a source of stress into a tool for growth.

> *Have you ever witnessed someone bounce back from tough feedback and display so much grace that they helped rally the team to victory?*

If we haven't trained ourselves to accept appropriate criticism, we may misinterpret it as a personal attack, triggering a fight-or-flight response. While this reaction was crucial for survival, it is less useful in today's workplace. We must learn to receive constructive criticism as intended: as guidance to assist us improve.

Understanding how to view criticism as constructive feedback instead of an attack on our character is essential for personal growth. By approaching feedback with curiosity and an open mindset, we can transform criticism from a source of fear into a valuable opportunity.

To facilitate this shift, consider the intention behind the feedback. Was it meant to be constructive, or did it arise from frustration? By analyzing the feedback and concentrating on actions instead of emotions, you can lessen the personal impact and reveal improvement areas. Although adapting this mindset requires practice, it enhances confidence and resilience, and self-regulation techniques are effective tools in this journey.

Self-regulation, which is all about managing our emotions during stressful moments, is such an important skill when it comes to receiving feedback constructively. Instead of snapping back defensively, self-regulation gives us a chance to take a breath and respond thoughtfully!

If you don't know where to begin, one of the simplest self-regulation techniques is deep breathing. Slow, intentional breaths reduce stress hormones and activate the parasympathetic nervous system, which counters our fight-or-flight response. A practice like "4-7-8" breathing involves inhaling for four counts, holding for seven, and exhaling for eight. Box breathing—breathing in a consistent four-count rhythm—also provides a steadying effect.

If you haven't tried this type of strategy, you'll be surprised at the results. Mindful breathing helps release physical tension by calming the mind and body and creating space between the moment of receiving criticism and the impulse to react.

Another way to interrupt your automatic responses to criticism is to take a mindful pause. This simple technique, sometimes called a "mindful moment," is an intentional pause that allows one to step back from an emotional reaction.

When you encounter criticism, taking a moment to pause can be as easy as a deep breath and becoming aware of any physical tension, like a clenched jaw or tight shoulders. This gentle awareness helps you focus on the present moment, allowing you to acknowledge those initial negative feelings—whether it's anger, hurt, or frustration—without any self-judgment.

When you take the time to recognize these feelings, your brain's initial emotional reaction becomes less intense, giving you the space to respond calmly. This little pause you create helps both parties approach tough conversations with a clearer mindset, fostering thoughtful discussions instead of quick reactions.

Unfortunately, as discussed earlier, negative internal dialogue often shapes how we respond to criticism. Cognitive reframing helps us challenge and reshape these internal narratives, shifting our mindset to more balanced, constructive thoughts.

Recognizing cognitive distortions such as personalization, catastrophizing, and overgeneralizing can assist in defusing the negative thoughts that intensify our emotional responses to feedback. For instance, when we personalize feedback, we perceive criticism as a judgment of our character instead of a critique of our actions. Likewise, catastrophizing exaggerates the possible repercussions of a minor issue, resulting in undue anxiety. On the other hand, overgeneralizing takes one mistake and applies it to a wider narrative of failure, which can often lead to feelings of discouragement

Reframing is all about taking a closer look at your thoughts and questioning whether they're really true. You might find it helpful to ask yourself, "What evidence do I have that supports or goes against this belief?" or think about what you would say to a friend in a similar situation. For instance, instead of telling yourself, "This feedback means I'm incompetent," reframing helps you discover the "opportunity to improve my approach." Cognitive reframing transforms criticism from something that depresses you down into an uplifting tool for growth, and paves the way for a constructive mindset.

Building our emotional intelligence, or EQ, will boost our resilience when we face criticism. EQ includes important qualities like self-awareness, empathy, and social skills, which help us navigate feedback more effectively. The journey starts with self-awareness, as it enables us to recognize and understand our emotional reactions. By identifying what triggers a defensive response and clarifying our unique strengths, we can create a balanced self-view that makes it much easier to accept negative feedback. Additionally, understanding our personal values is key; when we have a clear understanding of our core values, we can better prioritize feedback that supports our growth goals and gracefully let go of what doesn't serve us.

Empathy is the wonderful part of emotional intelligence that lets us see criticism through someone else's eyes, helping us feel less defensive. When we practice empathy, we think about where the feedback is coming from and what it means: Is the person trying to help, or are they feeling pressure that affects how they share their thoughts?

By considering the other person's viewpoint, we're more inclined to see feedback as helpful insights for our growth rather than as a personal attack. Empathy encourages us to respond with openness, and good social skills give us the ability to communicate in ways that keep our relationships strong, even when conversations get tough. In these feedback moments, actively listening without interrupting, asking questions for clarity, and showing appreciation, like saying, "Thank you for your input," demonstrates respect for the other person's perspective. This kind of approach builds trust and paves the way for positive connections and dialogue.

Mindfulness practices offer wonderful tools for managing stress and finding emotional balance. By being present in the moment, mindfulness helps us reduce overthinking and builds our resilience.

When we practice mindful listening during feedback sessions, we dedicate our full attention to the speaker's words, resisting the urge to plan our response while they're sharing. This approach nurtures deeper understanding and helps us avoid jumping to conclusions too quickly.

Mindful journaling, a practice where we jot down our thoughts and feelings after receiving feedback, gives us a helpful outlet for processing emotions. This thoughtful practice helps us sort through our feelings instead of letting them bubble under the surface. Another great mindfulness technique is visualization, where we picture a peaceful scene or a favorite place when criticism feels overwhelming. This simple mental exercise allows for a quick escape, reducing our emotional reactions and enabling us to return to the conversation feeling calm and with an open mind.

Meditation, especially when done regularly, can wonderfully enhance your ability to handle criticism by lowering stress levels. A simple meditation routine can be as easy as finding a comfy seat, tuning into your breath, and gently guiding your focus back to it whenever your thoughts drift away. At the end of your meditation, setting a positive intention, like being open to feedback, can really help strengthen a growth mindset.

Criticism, even when it's meant to help, can sometimes shake our confidence a bit. That's why it's so important to engage in practices that boost our self-worth and encourage self-compassion. One great way to do this is through positive self-talk.

By gently challenging those negative thoughts and swapping them out for uplifting affirmations like "I am capable of improvement," we nurture our self-compassion and realize just how much we can grow through feedback.

Taking a moment to recognize and celebrate our achievements, no matter how small also helps lift our confidence and balance out any negative feedback we receive. Finally, reminding ourselves of our strengths and past accomplishments can go a long way in reinforcing a positive mindset!

In our professional journeys, setbacks are unavoidable, and while criticism can be tough, they presents meaningful opportunities for growth.

Developing resilience in the face of criticism involves more than just accepting feedback; it requires viewing it as a road map for both personal and professional development. By practicing mindfulness, reframing negative thoughts, increasing emotional intelligence, and nurturing self-compassion, we can approach feedback from a position of strength instead of fragility. As we cultivate these abilities, criticism shifts from being a source of stress to becoming an essential resource for honing our skills and broadening our potential.

Resilience in dealing with criticism does not shield us from discomfort; rather, it enables us to welcome feedback with curiosity and an eagerness to grow. Through resilience, we transform feedback into a supportive ally that steers us toward enhanced confidence, flexibility, and success in our careers.

You can build resilience for yourself and others by embracing constructive feedback as a tool for growth. In doing so, you transform challenges into the learning opportunities that form the stepping stones to success.

Transforming the Organizational Culture

Transforming an organization plagued by toxic criticism is a formidable challenge. However, this issue cannot be overlooked; it is crucial, as neglecting it dooms the organization to fail.

A clear roadmap for cultural transformation is necessary to navigate this journey successfully. Enhancing corporate culture or substituting a toxic atmosphere with one rooted in positivity, respect, and open communication is no small task. Behaviors can become deeply ingrained, and territoriality often prevails. Yet, evolution is essential for an organization to thrive.

Have you ever been part of a team makeover so transformative that individual awards become team successes?

I have experienced all sorts of environments. I have wondered how people could behave so poorly. I have explained to teams how infighting of any sort is unacceptable, and used a simple analogy:

If you think of your organization as a team fighting to win in the marketplace and defending yourselves from competitors' attacks from every direction, then imagine you and your teammates forming a circle, and your weapons point outward. No one can penetrate the circle, and you are all protecting each other. However, if just one of you points your weapon inward, everyone will lose.

Every organization must have the same attitude toward eliminating infighting. Toxicity is the weapon being fired into the organization, weakening everyone and destroying any chance of success.

Once expectations are clarified, leaders must take action to eliminate toxicity and demonstrate their dedication to transforming the culture from one of negative criticism to one that embraces constructive and positive feedback. This requires a thoughtful strategy that includes clear communication guidelines, thorough training, and accountability for our behaviors, supported by strong leadership's commitment to cultural changes.

The first step in this transformation begins by defining and sharing standards for what constitutes acceptable behavior and communication.

These conduct guidelines should clearly define what respectful and constructive communication looks like, as well as what behaviors are not acceptable. While we might think that everyone knows what's unacceptable, it's surprising that even basic expectations need to be clearly articulated. It's important that these guidelines explain how we can create a supportive environment for giving and receiving helpful, growth-oriented feedback. Including examples of appropriate language, tone, and communication channels for feedback will be crucial to make this framework effective!

Once clear guidelines are established and everyone in the organization is made aware of them, it is critical that leadership sets the example and follows the guidelines. When leadership respects the same guidelines and expectations as every other member of the organization, everyone will participate and follow the accepted communication standard. People do so because they see and understand the benefits; everyone desperately wants to be heard and valued.

It should be intuitive that training people to deliver constructive feedback properly is crucial in shifting the organizational culture. Simply posting guidelines and hoping they will be observed or respected is naïve, because the solution to eliminating toxicity will not simply manifest itself magically. Just like anything else, change starts by teaching employees and leaders the skills to engage in positive communication practices. Training should focus on articulating feedback constructively and equally on how people should receive appropriate commentary positively.

If your team is used to a particular style of communication, and it has typically been negative, change will require more effort and also involve the development of mindful listening skills.

Remember: It's not just the speaker who needs to make adjustments and improve! We need to accept that the manner in which every one of us receives information is colored by prior experiences. Letting go of our innate defense mechanisms, which often lead us to react adversely to feedback, is essential for fostering positive change throughout the organization.

Many people have never experienced constructive feedback at home or work, so when constructive communication becomes an organizational focus, fear sets in as any required skills are nonexistent and need to be learned.

To learn how to accept constructive feedback, employees must first recognize that feedback is not a reflection of their character. Instead, it serves as guidance for their development and requires skills such as active listening, empathy, and emotional intelligence. One of the most difficult abilities to acquire is for the listener to show understanding by asking clarifying questions or explaining if they didn't find the feedback constructive. The phrase "I don't understand" can be empowering, highlighting a potential gap in training or the manager's communication. This underscores the necessity for feedback to be specific, actionable, and directed at clear tasks rather than personal traits.

Remember: People will never learn or adopt a new system by simply reading a memo.

If we want to transform our communication practices completely, it's important to embrace ongoing exercises that help everyone adapt to these changes. Regular practice not only boosts our skills and confidence but also makes it a breeze to give and receive constructive feedback!

Accountability plays a crucial role in making any cultural shift successful. It helps ensure that the new guidelines and training are truly put into action, rather than remaining just ideas. This means we need to monitor our communication styles, listen to how everyone interacts, and assess whether the guidelines are clear and the feedback process is adequate.

By having these standards in place, we can easily spot any toxic criticism and tackle those situations quickly and effectively!

When we need to address any issues after the guidelines are shared, it may involve personal coaching, formal warnings, or even more severe steps, depending on the behavior's impact. It's important that we apply accountability measures consistently and fairly at all levels of our organization, ensuring that everyone understands that we won't stand for toxic behavior. Occasionally, this may include dismissing high-performing team members whose actions are so concerning that we have to let them go.

Whether it's through openly denouncing bad behavior or making tough decisions like dismissal, we must clearly communicate that harmful actions against any individual won't be tolerated. If we don't, the message of inappropriate tolerance can spread throughout our organization. This situation can become tricky, especially when dealing with the difficult personalities whom we will soon define as "Assholes."

Deciding to dismiss an employee is a judgment call for leaders. Occasionally, slightly toxic behavior can be corrected and resolved through counseling. Yet, if problems continue despite these efforts, their termination becomes necessary.

When you are required to execute a termination due an individual's ongoing toxic behavior, you will have simultaneously failed and succeeded as a leader.

You have failed because you misjudged your ability to help them reform and because you refused to accept their unwillingness to grow. While it's important to acknowledge, there's also a silver lining: the rest of the organization will see two very positive things. First, you showed genuine empathy and a strong commitment to helping others succeed. Second, you invested your valuable time to support them and offered constructive feedback to help the person improve. Really, you've illustrated that everyone will be helped and also held to the same high standards of accountability. That's a powerful lesson for all!

For leaders to truly shine, it's essential that they embrace the power of constructive feedback in their everyday conversations. Being visible in their commitment, wholeheartedly joining in training sessions, and following the established communication guidelines are key steps they can take to foster a positive environment.

While it's important for leaders to be visible practicing and enforcing company policies, it's equally vital for them to proactively recognize and celebrate instances of constructive feedback within the organization. Acknowledging individual excellence not only reinforces that positive behavior but also shows employees that their hard work in adapting to the new culture is truly valued.

Fostering an atmosphere where respectful and constructive feedback prevails is essential for cultivating a culture of openness and trust. This can be achieved by promoting regular team discussions and feedback sessions, as well as establishing forums where employees feel safe to express their concerns and suggestions without fear of repercussions. While these forums don't require mandatory speaking, their success hinges on everyone knowing they can share their thoughts and that they will be acknowledged.

An environment that prioritizes openness and trust cultivates a sense of security among employees, making them more willing to give and receive feedback.

Transforming a culture affected by toxic criticism into one that cherishes constructive feedback necessitates a thorough and ongoing effort. However, it should quickly become apparent that these changes are welcomed and accepted by all.

By educating and applying positive communication techniques, organizations create more respectful and productive workspaces. Everyone aspires to work in uplifting environments because we all wish to contribute to our own growth and the organization's development.

Transforming culture begins with your commitment to foster respect, collaboration, and a shared vision for the future.

Learning How to Manage Others

It's not uncommon for staff members to be promoted into management roles without any training to prepare them properly.

Leading a team in a complex environment is challenging. While we can apply insights from team sports and school workgroups, the reality is that without prior training as a coach, it takes time to develop the skills required to manage others.

Have you ever watched a manager perform their job so skillfully that their team members were consistently earning their own promotions?

Unfortunately, over 75% of new managers surveyed reported having had no formal leadership training before their promotion. Without adequate training, anxieties become amplified, making it even harder for managers to unite diverse teams, achieve results, and retain talent in today's complex workplace pressure.

Building strong leadership skills swiftly is vital to your success as a manager. The organization believed in your potential and appointed you because your manager felt you were ready for a new challenge. Embracing flexible and dynamic approaches is critical to learning and developing your own style of core management skills. You'll find that skills for managing challenging personalities and creating a positive team atmosphere will be put to the test right away, so it's best to come prepared from day one!

Books like this can be beneficial in that regard. Managers can learn how to handle various personalities through the experiences of others. When faced with a challenging situation, you'll have the perspective needed to resolve issues and transform them into successful outcomes.

A highly effective method to enhance your management and leadership skills is to observe those you admire. Focus intently on their strategies for dealing with difficult personalities and how they interact with challenging team members to establish boundaries and alleviate tension. By recognizing leaders who adeptly handle intricate relationships, you can create a framework for resolving conflicts and gaining respect that resonates with your style and values.

Emulation serves as an excellent starting point. Seek out role models who excel in your organization's culture. Various workplaces appreciate distinct leadership styles; some emphasize assertiveness and agility, while others value thoughtfulness and humility. Pay attention to managers who effectively navigate your organization's unique cultural landscape. It's crucial to align with leaders who reflect your values since those demonstrating integrity and ethical behavior serve as better role models than those who achieve results at the expense of their principles.

Expanding your knowledge of leadership styles and conflict resolution is crucial, particularly for individuals aiming to refine their ability to handle challenging personalities. Immerse yourself in different leadership approaches by exploring books, podcasts, and industry blogs, emphasizing how each model tackles team dynamics and personality clashes. Seek out thought leaders who discuss modern workplace issues and provide perspectives on cultivating a collaborative team environment.

Having a solid support network can be truly invaluable! It's invaluable to your success to cultivate relationships with mentors who can provide you with thoughtful advice on managing workplace conflicts. A mentor from within your organization can share unique insights as you navigate different personalities, while external mentors can offer objective, unbiased perspectives on tackling challenging situations.

Exceptional leaders possess emotional intelligence and skillfully manage team dynamics, especially when facing challenging personalities. Effective handling of difficult team members requires keen awareness and flexibility, enabling leaders to ease tension while clearly defining expectations. With emotional intelligence, leaders can accurately assess situations, understand reactions, and modify their strategies accordingly.

One area for most managers can improve upon are their interpersonal sensitivity, especially during conflicts. It's important to know when to assert boundaries, when to listen, and how to communicate effectively without inflaming the situation. Observe how team members respond to your comments and pay attention to how seasoned leaders manage disagreement and encourage collaboration among different personalities. Building trust is crucial, so be available and regularly check in with your team, demonstrating real interest and responsiveness. Staying approachable and grounded can help minimize friction caused by challenging personalities.

When leading a team with diverse personalities, it is essential to maintain consistency and predictability in your approach. Team members must trust your leadership and feel assured about what to expect. However, being adaptable is also necessary; you should modify your style to accommodate different personality types. For instance, seasoned, high-performing individuals might require minimal oversight, whereas newer or more challenging personalities may benefit from a more structured and hands-on approach.

Balancing consistency with flexibility helps ensure that even the most difficult personalities can find common ground with you. By establishing firm boundaries and treating all team members fairly, you will create an environment where expectations are clear, and accountability is evenly applied.

People trust leaders who demonstrate fairness, so aim to be steady in your principles while agile in your interpersonal strategies.

Constructive feedback is a vital tool for your growth, particularly when learning how to manage challenging personalities. Even if your organization lacks formal feedback mechanisms, it's wise to proactively seek input from your team to understand how they perceive your leadership style. By doing so, you demonstrate your willingness to learn and improve. When you ask them to do the same, they are likely to be highly receptive, given your example.

Consistent feedback helps pinpoint areas for growth, particularly in team dynamics and challenging personalities. It also reveals how your actions affect the team's morale, enabling you to adjust your strategies with difficult individuals to enhance unity and reduce conflict. Leaders who proactively seek feedback demonstrate their dedication to ongoing yourself to learning, observing successful leaders, and enhancing your improvement and the cultivation of a supportive team environment.

Stepping into a leadership position without formal training can be tough, particularly when dealing with challenging personalities. By dedicating emotional intelligence, you can meet this challenge. Being prepared to manage difficult personalities directly and efficiently is crucial for fostering a positive and productive atmosphere, showcasing your leadership strength.

By committing to continuous learning, honing your methods, and gaining a profound understanding of various personalities, you'll adeptly manage intricate dynamics and lead with assurance. As you evolve, you will also prepare to mentor the upcoming generation of leaders, assisting them in addressing the challenges of team management with authenticity and resilience.

By mastering the skills of continuous learning and how to share feedback constructively, you'll master the key skills required to manage others and gain the ability to recognize the unique strengths of each member of your team.

The Role of HR in Managing Toxicity

It is easy to understand why toxic behavior in the workplace poses a serious threat to morale, productivity, and an organization's bottom line. HR professionals play a vital role in addressing, reducing, and ultimately preventing workplace toxicity by nurturing a culture filled with respect, transparency, and accountability.

With clear policies, engaging training, easy-to-access reporting mechanisms, and a heartfelt commitment to accountability, HR can build a supportive environment where every employee feels appreciated and heard. This chapter dives into how HR can actively combat workplace toxicity by developing thoughtful policies, creating interactive training programs, establishing welcoming reporting channels, and ensuring accountability at every level.

> *Have you ever worked with an HR team that felt less like a "resource" and more like your personal trainer, advocate, and growth advisor?*

Tackling workplace toxicity calls for a strategic, multi-faceted approach. The initial step for HR is to create clear and organized policies that specify what behaviors are acceptable and unacceptable within the company. Such policies lay the groundwork for the organization's cultural standards, clarifying expectations for employee interactions. This code of conduct needs to be communicated during the onboarding process and reviewed regularly to underscore its significance. By clearly identifying behaviors that qualify as harassment, bullying, discrimination, and other toxic actions, HR can establish well-defined boundaries that minimize misunderstandings and offer employees a sense of security.

In addition to defining acceptable conduct, HR must specify the repercussions for toxic behavior. These repercussions, ranging from progressive disciplinary measures to immediate actions, reflect the organization's commitment to fostering a respectful workplace. It is crucial for employees to recognize that toxic behaviors, whether shown by colleagues, managers, or senior leaders, will face consequences. Consistent application of these policies enhances their effectiveness. Trust in the organization's dedication to a respectful environment increases when employees observe that standards are uniformly upheld across all levels, from entry-level positions to executive roles.

Policies alone cannot eliminate toxicity; HR departments need to implement proactive training programs that foster a workplace culture defined by empathy, respect, and positive communication. These programs should address various aspects of workplace dynamics, including communication skills, emotional intelligence, conflict resolution, and stress management. For example, workshops focused on effective communication can teach employees to articulate their thoughts clearly and respectfully, while emotional intelligence training boosts their capacity to understand and relate to their colleagues. Regular training sessions establish a common language for discussing toxic behaviors and provide employees with the necessary tools for effective communication and conflict resolution.

Managers play a pivotal role in either preventing or perpetuating toxicity within teams. Accordingly, HR should focus on leadership training, providing managers with the tools needed to foster positive team dynamics and demonstrate respectful behavior. Team leaders often establish the norms for their groups, with employees seeking guidance from them on appropriate conduct. Training programs must help managers identify signs of toxicity, grasp the consequences of their actions, and learn to intervene effectively when problems occur. Leadership training should prioritize transparency and accountability, as managers who are open, approachable, and fair are more successful in preventing toxic behavior from taking root.

Alongside policies and training, HR needs to create accessible avenues for employees to report toxic behavior in a safe and confidential manner. In the absence of clear reporting options, employees might feel powerless to confront issues or fear retaliation for voicing their concerns. Providing various reporting methods, such as an anonymous hotline, a digital reporting system, or a specific HR representative, allows employees the flexibility to select the method they feel most at ease with. HR should actively promote these reporting avenues, consistently reminding employees that their concerns will be taken seriously and handled discreetly.

When toxic behavior is reported, HR must act quickly and consistently to investigate and resolve the problem. A swift response not only reassures the employee who reported the behavior but also underscores the organization's dedication to a safe and respectful workplace. Investigations should be carried out objectively, with HR professionals collecting evidence, interviewing relevant individuals, and documenting their findings. In instances of serious misconduct, HR might need to consult external experts or legal advisors to guarantee a fair and comprehensive investigation. Throughout this process, it is vital to maintain confidentiality to protect the privacy of everyone involved and prevent further harm.

After investigating a complaint, HR must ensure accountability by implementing the appropriate consequences as dictated by the organization's policies. Steady enforcement is vital to show that the company is serious about its standards. If consequences are not enforced, it can imply that toxic behavior is acceptable, particularly if the perpetrator occupies a position of authority. When employees see that some individuals can act toxic without facing consequences, it can lead to resentment and distrust, diminishing HR's efforts. Conversely, consistent enforcement strengthens the organization's commitment to fairness and cultivates a culture of accountability.

While policies, training, and reporting mechanisms are vital for HR in addressing toxicity, it is equally crucial to cultivate an organizational culture that prioritizes openness and transparency. HR must collaborate closely with leadership to exemplify desired behaviors and promote positive interactions. Employees need to feel they can raise concerns without fear of retaliation, making transparency essential. HR should create a psychologically safe environment where both positive and critical feedback can be shared constructively without repercussions. Maintaining open communication channels, such as regular employee feedback sessions or anonymous pulse surveys, allows HR to gauge the organization's culture and pinpoint areas that may require intervention.

Another step that HR must consider is the establishment of peer support programs or mentorship initiatives to promote healthy relationships among staff. Peer support programs enable employees to engage with each other, tackle challenges, and gain insights from common experiences, which helps alleviate the isolation frequently linked to toxic behavior. Meanwhile, mentorship initiatives can assist employees in their professional growth while cultivating a community and support network within the organization. By fostering these connections, HR can build a work environment where employees experience a feeling of belonging and accountability to each other, thereby decreasing the chances of toxic behavior.

Identifying the signs of toxicity early is crucial to stop its escalation. HR should track indicators of a toxic workplace, including rising absenteeism, high turnover rates, and regular burnout reports. Additionally, behaviors such as passive-aggressiveness, undermining coworkers, and excluding others from key discussions may indicate toxicity. By utilizing these indicators for assessments and talking with employees to uncover underlying issues, HR can tackle toxicity head-on, often resolving matters before they escalate into systemic problems.

Dealing with toxicity becomes especially difficult when it originates from senior leaders or top performers. In these situations, HR must navigate the sensitive balance between holding individuals accountable and managing organizational politics. Nonetheless, tackling toxic behavior at the leadership level is crucial since leaders who either embody or overlook such behavior send a harmful message throughout the organization. HR should push for a uniform approach, enforcing the same standards across the board, irrespective of an individual's position.

If senior leaders resist change, HR may need to collaborate with the executive team to consider alternative strategies, like leadership coaching or, in severe circumstances, removal from the organization.

HR must continuously evaluate how effective its strategies are in managing workplace toxicity. By analyzing data regarding employee engagement, turnover rates, and satisfaction levels both before and after implementing measures to address toxicity, HR can gauge the success of its initiatives and identify areas for improvement. Regularly collecting feedback from training sessions, reviewing reports on toxic behaviors, and conducting follow-up surveys will help HR enhance its strategies. A data-driven approach not only highlights the positive impact of these efforts but also emphasizes the importance of nurturing a healthy workplace culture for leadership and employees alike.

An often neglected component of managing toxicity is providing support to employees who are affected by it. While we frequently concentrate on addressing the perpetrators, we seldom conduct in-depth follow-ups with victims. The psychological toll of toxic behaviors—such as bullying, harassment, or exclusion—can be profound, especially for those with prior traumas. HR should ensure that staff have access to resources like counseling services and conflict resolution workshops. Utilizing employee assistance programs to aid employees in recovering from the long-term effects of negative childhood experiences can yield tremendous benefits. These hidden wounds may be concealed, yet they inflict considerable pain and suffering, impacting both personal and professional lives in numerous ways. By showing commitment to employee well-being following incidents of toxicity, HR fosters trust and demonstrates that the organization values a respectful and supportive environment.

When managing toxicity, it's important for HR to connect their strategies with the core values and mission of the organization. Companies that champion integrity, respect, and collaboration are more likely to create a warm and positive culture. HR can help reinforce these values through regular communication—like newsletters, team meetings, and engaging internal campaigns. For instance, recognizing employees who embody these values or celebrating teams that show collaboration and respect can really inspire those desired behaviors. By aligning anti-toxicity efforts with the organization's mission, HR can make building a positive workplace culture a key part of the company's identity, encouraging everyone to support each other in accountability.

HR plays a vital role in shaping our workplace atmosphere, working tirelessly to manage and prevent toxicity. By developing thoughtful policies, engaging training programs, and clear reporting channels, HR helps foster an environment where everyone feels safe and valued. With a focus on transparency, trust, and open communication, we can work together to keep negativity at bay and nurture a Workplace where everyone can flourish. It's not just about avoiding pitfalls; it's about building a culture that empowers each of us to thrive in a respectful and inclusive setting. With careful policy design, consistent support, and a shared commitment to our core values, HR can truly elevate our workplace culture, making it a healthier and more productive space for all.

HR thrives when it fosters an environment of fairness and empathy to ensure that every voice is heard and every challenge is met with dignity.

From Theory into Practice

One of the most helpful ways to understand the impact of poorly delivered criticism on organizations is by looking at examples many of us can relate to. It's an unfortunate pattern in history that mistakes tend to repeat themselves. Unfortunately, this also provides us with plenty of examples to explore, highlighting not only the errors made but also the ways the companies chose to respond.

> *Have you ever dealt with someone who quoted management theories so often you wondered if they were trying to earn royalties on the buzzwords?*

> or

> *Have you ever seen someone take a management theory and turn it into an everyday practice so seamlessly that it felt like magic?*

We all crave the manager who executes on supporting excellence without fanfare and leads by example.

One very well-documented organizational failure and recovery occurred at Google in 2017. As a result of various posts and allegations, which included allegations that certain managers would give employees negative feedback in a public and demeaning way, the company responded and took action.

Google's response was swift and decisive for a company of any size. The company's CEO, Sundar Pichai, took responsibility and sent an email to all employees acknowledging the seriousness of the allegations and apologized to any employees who had been mistreated. But he did not just acknowledge the problems, he took action and announced several steps that Google would be taking to address the problem and the specific allegations. This included terminating managers who were found to have been using toxic methods to deliver feedback.

The attention surrounding the posts and allegations quickly and profoundly affected the workplace culture at Google. Some individuals felt relief that the inappropriate behavior was brought to light, while others were appalled by its existence. Recognizing and addressing a genuine issue is always productive.

Fortunately, Google's executive team understood that the feedback stemmed from a desire for improvement, not malicious intent. Consequently, the company's robust response and proactive measures illustrated that Google's leadership was dedicated to progressive management and fostering a more positive and supportive work environment for their employees.

In response to the allegations, a reporting system was established to address micromanagement and humiliation. This system has proven effective, simplifying the process for employees to report any instances of abuse. Additionally, Google acknowledged the necessity of training for managers on how to deliver constructive feedback. This training emphasizes the importance of being aware of the effects of their words and encourages ongoing improvement in communication methods with employees.

The assessment of Google's culture prompted several crucial changes. Many of these adjustments had been long overdue, indicating that the company's rapid growth had surpassed its capacity to adapt internal processes appropriately. The notion that "this is how it's always been done" became unacceptable. For instance, Google's leadership acknowledged that internal communication regarding various issues was insufficient and many policies were outdated. Consequently, the company introduced a new policy mandating regular one-on-one meetings between managers and their employees to foster stronger relationships and ensure clear communication.

Google and similar companies utilize business tools to pinpoint challenges ahead of time; however, many often miss the chance to gauge internal sentiment, leaving them unaware of potentially serious issues. Thankfully, the feedback system developed by Google to gather confidential staff input has been made available to the public. This remarkable resource should inspire leaders across organizations to explore how they can adopt a similar system, enabling their teams to provide valuable insights.

This is crucial because, while organizations must thoughtfully implement systems for constructive feedback, the challenges at Google also underscored the necessity for an extra layer to guarantee compliance. Ideally, such systems would be unnecessary. However, since we do not exist in that ideal environment, a compliance measurement system proves to be essential.

To implement their feedback loop, Google now asks employees to fill out a thirteen-question manager feedback on a semi-annual basis.

In line with their commitment to transparency and continual improvement, they provide a self-assessment and an anonymous peer assessment tool on their website. Feedback responses are kept confidential, and managers receive a report featuring anonymized aggregated feedback along with the verbatim responses to open-ended questions found at the end of the form. The initial eleven questions prompt employees to indicate their agreement or disagreement with various statements about their manager using a five-point Likert scale, which aids managers and their HR supervisors in gauging communication effectiveness with their teams.

The questions are simple. However, the responses provide clear and actionable insights to help managers adjust their approach to better suit their staff's needs.

> 1) My manager gives me actionable feedback that helps me improve my performance.
>
> 2) My manager does not "micromanage" (i.e., get involved in details that should be handled at other levels).
>
> 3) My manager shows consideration for me as a person.
>
> 4) The actions of my manager show that they value the perspective I bring to the team, even if it is different from their own.
>
> 5) My manager keeps the team focused on our priority results/deliverables.
>
> 6) My manager regularly shares relevant information from their manager and senior leaders.
>
> 7) My manager has had a meaningful discussion with me about career development in the past six months.
>
> 8) My manager communicates clear goals for our team.
>
> 9) My manager has the technical expertise (e.g., coding in Tech, selling in Global Business, accounting in Finance) required to manage me effectively.
>
> 10) I would recommend my manager to other Googlers.
>
> 11) I am satisfied with my manager's overall performance as a manager.

The final two questions are open-ended and allow for the staff to write longer responses that explain deeper feelings and observations:

1) What would you recommend your manager keep doing?

2) What would you have your manager change?

Management should consistently ask itself and its employees critical questions. It's important to acknowledge that while we evaluate our team, they also judge our abilities as leaders. Without straightforward feedback, individuals may remain unaware of their communication mistakes with peers, colleagues, and direct reports. Each of us has distinct mannerisms, and we might not realize how our idiosyncrasies can obscure or distort the messages we communicate.

By actively pursuing constructive feedback from those we engage with every day, we can gain insights into ourselves and understand what changes we need to implement for improvement. You don't have to alter your core self, but you may need to adjust how you deliver your messages at times. We all have room for growth.

In business, we all recognize the adage, "you can't manage what you don't measure." Likewise, we cannot effectively manage ourselves or enhance our skills without the insights gained from honest and objective feedback. Feelings of being unappreciated or undervalued can surface at any level within an organization. It is challenging for the C-Suite to balance confidentiality while addressing these concerns, yet it is essential. Even a company's board must engage in these conversations as part of their ongoing relationship with leadership. Failing to do so neglects the emotional demands of the organization's leaders; if the board remains solely focused on financial performance, the board risks creating a toxic culture.

Other companies have learned and can continue to learn lessons from Google's experience. It is guaranteed that every company will face similar situations in one form or another. Best they are prepared.

Human behavior is rarely unique or original. Bad behavior is simply more obvious for everyone to see. Companies need to be mindful that problems will undoubtedly occur if proactive measures are not implemented and that even with every possible mechanism in place, there will always be another new problem.

Neglecting to establish safeguards against employee abuse is unacceptable. When claims of misconduct emerge, businesses need to react swiftly and firmly. The best initial step in assessing a situation is introspection. Reflect on how you wish to be treated, and approach the allegation from that viewpoint. Everyone deserves to be engaged with the same level of civility and professionalism that you expect for yourself.

For a system to be effective, it's crucial that everyone is aware of its existence and that the company is dedicated to prioritizing employee welfare. Accountability means companies should set up secure and confidential whistleblower systems that allow employees to report any misconduct. These systems are not limited to personal grievances; individuals need avenues to report abuses and other inappropriate actions such as theft, vandalism, fraud, bribery, and personal harm. Addressing these toxic behaviors is essential for a successful whistleblower system.

Like anything else, merely proclaiming a new system is inadequate. Companies need to continuously assess their culture to pinpoint and tackle emerging systemic issues. They also can't just react by implementing escalation procedures when problems surface. Doing so fosters a culture that tolerates destructive behaviors. When a concern is raised, leadership must conduct a thorough investigation into the complaint and document the findings to show a clear understanding of the challenges involved.

However, if an incident reveals a flaw in the system, failing to act while an investigation is underway is detrimental and unacceptable. For instance, if a company learns that a product was stolen from a location due to blind spots in security camera coverage, there is no reason to postpone addressing the theft. The fact remains that the security system was insufficient and requires enhancement.

When allegations of abuse or misconduct arise, it is inappropriate to force the involved parties to collaborate during the investigation. The correct strategy is to keep them apart. It's vital to assure that both parties believe they will be treated fairly; this is key to preserving staff trust in the process and management. If not, employees might view the procedures as inequitable and may be reluctant to report issues in the future.

Regardless of whether an allegation of impropriety or abuse is proven correct, it serves as a reminder that companies can't just implement systems; they must demonstrate commitment to the values.

Companies also need to establish systems that consistently re-evaluate their initiatives. In the absence of such systems, complacency can take hold, leading to the emergence of new tactics intended to undermine the policies' goals. Consequently, management may end up merely responding to issues rather than proactively preventing them.

No system is ever good enough. We should never be complacent and believe we have finished improving. If we believe we have become good enough, we are complacent, and complacency will destroy any organization.

Putting your ideas into action is your opportunity to turn aspirations into reality, paving the way for meaningful growth and transformative success.

Managing your Manager

When you join an organization, you expect and intend to contribute your best qualities and make a positive impact. Regardless of your position, your presence always matters, and it's the collective responsibility of all employees, not only management, to foster a healthy work environment. Improving a difficult situation necessitates conscious efforts from many individuals.

Just as leaders should adopt best practices in corporate culture, organizations need to offer strategies that help employees build constructive upward relationships.

> *Have you ever helped guide a manager who was struggling with a difficult situation so that it felt like you were coaching them?*

Regardless of an individual's commitment to maintaining ideal behavior, everyone can exhibit difficult behaviors occasionally. It is therefore crucial to empower employees to advocate for themselves and establish boundaries without fearing conflict, fostering an environment of open communication and mutual respect.

Employees play the most significant role in transforming the workplace, not merely due to their numbers but also because a healthy work environment requires widespread accountability and appropriate behavior from everyone. Their influence extends beyond mutual encouragement; they can also assist in steering their managers in the right direction.

But where to start?!?

In the past, feedback in the workplace often felt like a one-way street, with managers sharing their insights while employees listened. This method was rooted in an outdated, top-down approach, where managers were thought of as the only experts, and employees were expected to follow directions without question. Nowadays, modern management styles are all about encouraging open communication, where two-way feedback and collaboration thrive. Great managers in today's organizations genuinely value input from their employees and strive to provide feedback in a constructive and supportive way.

The impact of feedback on productivity hinges on its delivery method. Conventional management approaches that rely on one-sided, critical feedback, are proven to harm productivity. Reflecting on our school experiences makes this clear. Students who experience relentless criticism from a teacher tend to be less motivated and produce lower-quality work. Conversely, instructors who offer constructive guidance empower their students to thrive and succeed.

The following table summarizes some of the key differences between traditional and modern management styles when it comes to feedback:

Traditional Management Style	**Modern Management Style**
Feedback is one-way, from manager to employee.	Feedback is two-way, between manager and employee.
Feedback is often based on a top-down hierarchy, where managers are seen as the experts, and employees are expected to follow their instructions.	Feedback is based on collaboration and mutual respect.
Feedback can be critical and judgmental.	Feedback is constructive and supportive.
Feedback is often focused on past performance.	Feedback is focused on both past and future performance.

Even the most innovative managers are highly flawed individuals, just like you, me, and everyone else. While each person's flaws may vary, everyone can benefit from the guidance of those around them to improve! Assisting a manager in recognizing their own shortcomings offers the exciting opportunity to enhance communication skills and practice delivering constructive criticism.

When you help your manager improve, you lead up! Leading up demonstrates your leadership potential, and signals your desire for advancement.

One great way for any employee to grow is by asking for constructive feedback. This shows a genuine commitment to personal development and encourages positive discussions. When employees seek feedback, they truly demonstrate that they value their manager's insights. This not only boosts the manager's sense of worth but also fosters a more comfortable environment for open communication for everyone.

To effectively seek feedback, employees need to specify the areas for input. For instance, an employee might say, "I want to enhance my presentation skills. Could you provide feedback on my upcoming presentation?" When the employee presents next, their manager will pay closer attention in light of this request and engage in an insightful conversation afterward.

When seeking feedback, it's crucial to stay open-minded to what you might hear, even if it's negative! This involves listening to the feedback attentively without interrupting or getting defensive. However, if the tone is inappropriate, that should not be tolerated.

If the feedback is unclear and fails to provide direction for improvement, you should ask clarifying questions to grasp the message fully. In life, acknowledging when we don't understand something is important, as is requesting further details; for instance, asking, "Could you provide an example of what you mean?" This approach also gently signals to your manager the need to enhance their feedback for it to be actionable. In this way, you are once again leading up!

Employees can also demonstrate constructive behavior by offering their managers constructive feedback and providing critiques in a productive manner. When giving feedback, it's essential for employees to be specific, timely, and respectful, just as they would want to be treated themselves. Emphasizing behavior rather than personal traits is key. For instance, you could say, "I saw your presentation to the client yesterday, it was really good, but I was most impressed by how you managed people's difficult questions."

Just as we appreciate our managers being patient with us, it's important to understand that it may also take them some time to become aware of their own subconscious behaviors and make the necessary adjustments. While we should never expect or accept toxic or unacceptable behavior, we must all strive to be patient with more subtle issues, provided the manager shows a genuine commitment to improving.

While there is no excuse for poor behavior, it's important to acknowledge that everyone has flaws. If a person is striving to improve, they warrant our support. As previously stated, this path of growth and development is ongoing!

Kindness and generosity are virtues. Unfortunately, weaker individuals commonly seek to take advantage of others and abuse these virtues. Please note the emphasis on the word abuse. When abuse occurs, the damage can be irreparable.

It's important to remember that even with all the goodwill and generosity in the world, some people may not be open to feedback. When this happens and it affects someone else's ability to do their job, we need to find other ways to help. For instance, just like Google has created a feedback survey system to encourage growth, we should have alternative options available if talking directly isn't possible. If you're not able to get through to your manager or if you prefer a more private way to share your thoughts, please know that the HR team is there to listen and support you. They're ready to provide guidance and assistance or step in to help build those crucial connections that can lead to everyone's success.

Criticism is a natural part of any workplace. It will either happen in constructive and positive ways to support growth or in ways that harm employee morale, productivity, and retention.

No matter our role in an organization, we are all contributors. It's your choice what aspects of the business you will contribute to, but it is always your responsibility to contribute positively.

Managing up is your opportunity to lead from any position, fostering stronger relationships and rallying the team to share accountability for success.

Reciprocal Constructive Criticism

It is not surprising that a study by the Society for Human Resource Management (www.shrm.org) found that companies with a culture of two-way feedback have higher employee engagement and productivity than companies without this form of culture. The study also found that companies with a culture of two-way feedback have less turnover.

Have you ever been part of a feedback exchange so positive it felt like a high-five for your professional growth?

Critically, the study summarized that this strong culture has three pillars that lead to greater success.

"When an organization has a strong culture, three things happen: Employees know how top management wants them to respond to any situation, employees believe that the expected response is the proper one, and employees know that they will be rewarded for demonstrating the organization's values." shrm.org

No matter how we consider criticism, its impact on organizational culture is complex.

Ongoing, two-way feedback strengthens relationships and improves teamwork. By promoting a culture where both employees and managers are open to receiving feedback, we support mutual growth and accountability, enhancing overall organizational health.

When handled effectively, criticism can serve as the groundwork for the core values, beliefs, attitudes, and behaviors shared within an organization. A culture characterized by clear and open communication influences how employees engage with each other and outside stakeholders, directly impacting the organization's overall performance and effectiveness.

Understanding and cultivating the appropriate organizational culture is essential for managerial success. A robust and positive culture not only boosts employee engagement but also fosters a better atmosphere both at home and in the workplace, leading to significant improvements in job performance and overall organizational success.

Creating a positive culture requires committed leadership, clear communication, and a thoughtful alignment of policies and practices with the values we cherish and behaviors we aspire to embody for lasting success. Navigating the challenges of fostering the right culture calls for a strategic and inclusive mindset. This approach not only keeps our culture vibrant but also ensures it aligns beautifully with our organization's goals and celebrates our diversity.

Employees who feel valued and supported by their managers are far more likely to be engaged and to produce high-quality work. When companies fail to create a culture of two-way feedback, they sow the seeds of their destruction by permitting a Culture of Fear to take root within the organization.

Reciprocal feedback strengthens trust and collaboration and helps to create a culture where everyone is invested in each other's growth.

The Culture of Fear and Team Morale

A culture of fear is characterized by persistent anxiety, uncertainty, and apprehension among employees. It diverts their attention from genuine performance to concerns about job security, performance evaluations, and how they are perceived, rather than actual performance. Fear suppresses creativity, lowers morale, and heightens turnover rates.

A culture marked by negativity severely harms both individual and team morale. The ongoing fear of criticism or humiliation decreases staff trust in one another and hampers effective collaboration, ultimately leading to reduced productivity.

> *Have you ever dealt with a workplace so ruled by fear that even the coffee machine seemed nervous?*

> *or*

> *Have you ever been part of a team that replaced fear with so much support and encouragement that even regular visitors' morale skyrocketed?*

It's important to recognize that fear isn't limited to just the staff. Managers can also experience discomfort or fear when engaging with peers or subordinates in such environments. When these feelings arise, the first step is to reflect on your interactions with the other person to understand the source of that discomfort. Often, seeking input or help from a colleague or supervisor can be beneficial, as either your concerns or the other person's behavior might indicate an underlying issue that needs attention.

In rapidly expanding early-stage companies, it's common for many corporate systems and guidelines to remain underdeveloped. Both junior and experienced staff must adapt to varying workplace cultures, depending on their backgrounds. For instance, a manager accustomed to traditional hierarchical management may face challenges with assertive team members who favor a modern, mutual feedback approach. While neither party may engage in inappropriate interactions, their style of communication will likely differ greatly and result in misunderstandings and distrust.

At times, two individuals may struggle to adapt swiftly enough to prevent conflicts, which can become unavoidable if they fail to grasp the subtleties of their differing communication styles and behaviors. Such conflicts hinder growth, innovation, and productivity; rather, they foster resentment that stifles communications.

When communication is stifled, it rarely affects just the relationship between two people. This can create a ripple effect that impacts their teams and can lead to a toxic atmosphere. Much like negative feedback, if left unchecked, it can poison the entire workplace. Whether the issue arises from a manager's interactions with one person or many, recognizing the factors that foster a culture of fear is crucial for organizations aiming to build a more positive, supportive, and productive environment.

One of the main factors that can foster a culture of fear is leadership that leans towards being authoritarian or punitive. Similar to the toxicity discussed earlier, this environment is often characterized by negative criticism. When managers adopt a top-down or command-and-control approach, emphasizing strict rule-following and focusing primarily on immediate consequences for mistakes, it tends to stifle creativity and innovation, ultimately creating a fearful atmosphere.

I've met businesspeople who believe their staff should jump and eagerly ask, "How high?" when asked to. Employees under this type of management feel like they are constantly being scrutinized and evaluated, which naturally leads to a reluctance to take risks or voice their thoughts. This fear increases when leaders resort to fear-based motivation, suggesting or explicitly stating that job security hinges on meeting certain expectations, which can often feel unrealistic.

The absence of open communication combined with a manager's practice of disclosing only essential details fosters fear. Employees should be informed about information that impacts their performance or career. When important details are kept secret, or when decisions, policies, and expectations lack clarity, it creates uncertainty and anxiety among staff.

The same holds true for management when staff don't communicate issues promptly.

This lack of transparency is particularly damaging when it comes to organizational changes, such as restructuring, layoffs, or management changes.

Changes are inevitable and often indicate positive development. Nevertheless, when employees lack clarity about their job security, rumors and misinformation can spread rapidly, heightening feelings of insecurity and anxiety among staff. In such scenarios, many begin to look for alternatives.

While operational adjustments like layoffs are never pleasant, they can serve a beneficial purpose for a company, helping safeguard the jobs of those who remain and aligning operations with a new context. Anticipation of layoffs can trigger fear-driven behavior; however, when employees receive honest reassurances about their job security, that fear tends to fade away.

Open and ongoing communication helps ease the anxiety surrounding the unknown. In many workplaces, it's natural for individuals to feel nervous as quarterly reviews approach. However, when communication is handled well within the organization, you should never be caught off guard by anything discussed during your quarterly or performance review. Instead, the only surprise should be an unexpected promotion!

If a performance review reveals unexpected information, it indicates that the manager and organization could improve their communication in-between meetings.

Performance reviews that concentrate solely on issues will foster a culture of fear. Employees seek to understand the ways they can improve because everyone has a desire to grow. Michael Jordan practiced shooting baskets every day, not because he wasn't already the best, but because he recognized there still was potential for improvement.

Feedback that highlights only problems diminishes employee motivation; when workers perceive their evaluations as unjust or primarily punitive rather than as chances for development, simply scheduling a review instills anxiety. This anxiety results in short-term thinking, causing employees to prioritize evading negative feedback and evaluations over their long-term growth and potential contributions to the organization.

Workplace stress extracts a staggering toll on both employees and employers alike. While some stress can motivate productivity toward defined goals, excessive and prolonged stress reduces performance, satisfaction, and retention.

Moreover, the cascading costs of untreated employee stress take a significant financial toll on organizations. Evaluating and mitigating unnecessary stress through supportive policies promises to substantially improve productivity, morale, and profitability.

To properly assess the costs associated with toxicity, it's essential to first examine its origins in workplace stress. Stress arises when employees experience feelings of being overwhelmed, lack a healthy work-life balance, fear job loss or criticism, or struggle to manage excessive workloads.

The American Psychological Association's 2020 Work and Wellbeing Survey reveals that over 70% of employees identify work as a primary source of stress. Research shows that four out of five employees experience the impact of workplace stress, which often follows them home. This stress can then affect their families and may lead to abusive behaviors that have lasting consequences for children, who may repeat these patterns when they become parents. This underscores why addressing toxicity and stress in the workplace is vital: to disrupt the cycle of abuse that impacts numerous individuals.

Not all stress is bad, and we should recognize the difference between productive stress and the harmful stress that stems from abuse. Short-term stress can effectively drive immediate productivity, but when stress becomes chronic, it negatively impacts both physical and mental health.

The Mayo Clinic has conducted extensive research on this matter, revealing that long-term stress exposure makes employees susceptible to problems such as depression, sleep disorders, cognitive impairment, indecisiveness, and burnout syndrome. Furthermore, psychoneuroimmunology research establishes a connection between chronic stress and weakened immune systems alongside inflammatory responses. Instead of being merely a morale issue, untreated stress among employees inflicts physical harm on their health.

In addition to harming well-being, the cascade effect of untreated employee stress also hits the bottom line through plummeting workplace productivity and skyrocketing costs in four key areas:

1) Turnover
2) Healthcare expenditures
3) Absenteeism
4) Presenteeism

Research consistently shows that stressed employees often leave their jobs at alarming rates. The 2001 study by Hoel, Sparks, and Cooper, published in the International Labour Organisation, revealed that 40% of all employee turnover stems from unhealthy stress levels in the workplace. This issue can be addressed through improved management practices and proactive measures that include enhanced healthcare options, training, and initiatives aimed at reducing toxicity.

A 40% turnover rate caused by any single factor is unacceptable. Moreover, we must acknowledge that many individuals experience distress quietly, resulting in a much higher affected rate. The tendency to resign rather than endure stress significantly impacts a company's finances due to lost productivity and replacement costs. Flash's landmark analysis in 1997 determined that turnover costs can average between 120% to 200% of the salary of the departing employee, factoring in lost productivity, recruiting, onboarding, and training expenses.

The math is clear. By not paying attention to stress, a company pushes talented team members out the door and sabotages net bottom line profitability by upwards of 10%!

In addition to the turnover issue, stressed employees who remain in their positions will incur significantly higher healthcare costs. This is a self-inflicted wound on the organization's bottom line causing the cost of employee benefit plans to rise.

A 1999 publication from the National Institute for Occupational Safety and Health indicates that workplace stress is linked to 50% higher medical expenses. This relates to factors like stress-related insomnia combined with high caffeine intake or self-medication with tobacco and alcohol, which lead to physical decline and increased healthcare spending. Consequently, chronic stress diverts healthcare resources from providing actual care to addressing the resulting health issues.

Data review clearly shows that stressed and distressed employees take more sick days. A peer-reviewed study by Munce, Stansfeld, et al. in 2007 found that depression, frequently caused by ongoing stress, is the leading cause of absenteeism. When employees face mental health issues, they are more likely to miss work due to both psychological (such as needing counseling) and physical factors (like illnesses resulting from weakened immune systems). Consequently, stressed teams tend to miss work more often. The NIOSH reports that large companies lose about $3.6 million each year due to absenteeism related to untreated employee mental health issues and stress.

When stress affects employees, it leads to a decline in their productivity and create distractions due to disengagement at work. According to a study by Johnson, Westerfield et al. published in the Journal of Occupational and Environmental Medicine back in 2009, presenteeism - when individuals come to work but aren't fully engaged - can be more expensive than absenteeism. While absent employees don't interrupt their colleagues, those who come in but can't fully participate due to their health struggles can hinder productivity. The study highlights that for every $0.47 companies invest in treating underlying psychological issues, they lose another $0.53 due to the disengagement that stems from unresolved conditions.

After looking into the psychological effects and financial consequences of workplace stress, it's important to discuss practical steps to address these root causes. The evidence is clear; every organization should take note! While even the healthiest environments and most positive leaders can't completely erase the stressors that come with high performance, they can definitely help reduce and eliminate the negativity that leads to toxic stress.

The evolution of modern motivational theory, starting from Maslow's hierarchy of needs to Herzberg's Two Factor model, illustrates that employee priorities evolve in a clear sequence. Employees must first secure basic requirements such as adequate compensation, career development opportunities, job stability, work-life balance, and overall wellness before they can pursue purpose or self-actualization at work. Effective leaders create an environment where employees can thrive without the worry about these essential needs or being burdened by excessive workloads that exceed the available workforce or resources. Competent managers continuously assess resource limitations and the capacity of their teams to ensure that there is harmony between labor supply and demand, preventing any employee from facing overwork or excessive personal strain.

Of course, with work-from-home arrangements muddying separation and constant connectivity blurring work-life lines, management must also proactively establish new rules and train supervisors to model and respect healthy boundaries.

Entrepreneurs often find themselves tackling issues and ideas at all hours, whenever something needs immediate attention. While it's common to send out inquiries and instructions late into the night, great managers know that without clear boundaries, this can lead to confusion. It's important for everyone on the team to understand that they can take a break from responding to emails during those odd hours.

As an entrepreneur who sometimes juggles the challenges of ADHD, I have a tendency to handle tasks whenever inspiration strikes. However, those who collaborate with me quickly realize that I truly don't want or expect anyone to reply to emails outside of regular work hours. Just because I'm working at unconventional times doesn't mean anyone else should feel pressured to do the same!

Fortunately, email scheduling tools have rendered this a simpler issue to manage!

While impossible a few years ago, the ability to schedule emails is a blessing for me and those who collaborate with me; now, these notes can accumulate and only be delivered during appropriate times. We all have our quirks and must find ways to operate within environments that maximize our effectiveness. However, while we need to model the best behavior for those around us, we also can't suppress the idiosyncrasies that make us effective.

Outside of emergencies, the expectation needs to be that no matter when a manager sends an email, staff should only respond during regular work hours. Expecting otherwise is neither recommended nor appreciated.

Managers who send late-night or weekend emails demanding subordinates work outside regular hours undermine morale and retention by demonstrating a lack of respect for their teams' personal lives and needs. The odd-hour habit either reflects the individual's abnormal work schedule or workaholic tendencies stemming from a lack of balance and healthy stress-coping outlets.

Individuals who work unusual hours—without working too many—definitely deserve a unique understanding compared to workaholics. Often, these schedules simply reflect how someone is juggling their other responsibilities or engagements. For instance, a single parent might adjust their timetable to better meet their child's needs. This sometimes means they're away during traditional work hours, but they'll gladly pick up their tasks later in the day or evening.

A sales team member with clients in various time zones will also adapt to their schedules accordingly and should feel at ease with modifying their schedules, not simply adding more to their plates. It's been demonstrated repeatedly that high achievers excel when they have the opportunity to unplug from work to prevent burnout. Effective management prioritizes deliverables and results rather than merely tracking the number of hours worked.

Wise corporate stewardship entails caring for the sustainable deployment of human capital. People are not machines, and they need to be managed and supported accordingly!

Those who think that "stress is 10% circumstance and 90% reaction" are insensitive to their own contribution to the stress around them. Elements such as harsh leadership, criticism without context, incivility, harassment, and bullying foster detrimental stress by establishing hostile environments. Along with demonstrating supportive behavior, executive leaders and HR professionals actively coach against and confront toxic dynamics that undermine team unity.

Psychologically safe cultures are necessary to allow people to engage in more vulnerable dialogue without fear of retaliation. By providing everyone with a safe environment, we can resolve tension before it festers.

Some managers rationalize untreated employee stress as an inevitable by-product of the elite performance expectations built into their culture. This runs completely counter to reality. Any excessive demands they push on staff, believing it is motivational, will only result in accelerated resignation rates as they push personnel past sustainable limits.

Conversely, data reveals that reducing stress produces better health, satisfaction, creative thinking, and sustainable effort over longer durations.

Building a healthy workplace environment that supports and encourages high-performance levels without toxicity entails reconceiving many elements previously held as fixed or non-negotiable legacy practices. As part of that reevaluation, fealty to any legacy practices that are understood by as "it's always been done this way" must be the first sacred cows dispensed with.

Ultimately, as stewards of people rather than just managers of talent, management is called upon to deploy and develop human capital in a sustainable manner, allowing individuals and institutions alike to flourish. Sustainable management requires that we continuously assess stress loads to avoid burnout. While limited periods of heightened urgency may require working above standard capacity, allowing these strains to become the status quo only serves to water the seeds of stress, toxicity, and turnover.

While stress is a normal physiological response, and we know that not all stress is counterproductive, it becomes problematic when it becomes chronic or excessive.

When employee stress becomes chronic and unresolved, it not only impacts individual health but also places a heavy burden on organizations. This leads to increased costs associated with voluntary terminations, medical claims, absenteeism, and presenteeism, ultimately resulting in more than a trillion dollars lost in productivity each year. Tackling this issue is essential for everyone's well-being and the overall health of the organization.

In the workplace, negative stress arises from high workloads, tight deadlines, interpersonal conflicts, toxic criticism, lack of control over work, and job insecurity. Employees who experience prolonged periods of stress will experience burnout. The onset of burnout from physical, emotional, and mental exhaustion occurs gradually, and at every step along the way, productivity decreases. What we recognize as burnout, when the employee steps away, is just the final step. The damage was done months and years prior.

A significant study in the "Journal of Applied Psychology" revealed that lower productivity and reports of decreased work performance, diminished cognitive abilities, and increased absenteeism will precede any reports of burnout. It's unfortunate for all involved that the problems are addressed and excused as the employee's problem, not a symptom of an larger organizational issue. If one employee is feeling the effects, all employees are sharing in them.

A critical aspect of the relationship between workplace stress and productivity is its effect on mental health. Research in occupational health psychology consistently indicates that elevated stress levels can cause or exacerbate mental health issues, including anxiety and depression. A study published in the "Journal of Occupational Health Psychology" highlighted that these mental health conditions, as anticipated, also result in reduced productivity, as individuals affected experience greater challenges with concentration, decision-making, tasks, and the maintenance of relationships.

Workplace stress adversely impacts employees physiologically, which consequently affects productivity. Chronic stress is linked to various physical health issues, such as cardiovascular diseases, musculoskeletal disorders, and weakened immune systems. These health problems can result in higher rates of absenteeism and presenteeism (working while unwell), as indicated by research in the "Journal of Occupational and Environmental Medicine." Notably, presenteeism is recognized as a critical yet frequently overlooked factor contributing to decreased productivity. Employees may attend work but lack the mental presence necessary for meaningful contribution.

The impact of stress on productivity also extends to team dynamics and overall organizational performance. People operating in high-stress environments consistently deal with poor communication, conflict, and a breakdown in teamwork, as found in studies published in "Organizational Behavior and Human Decision Processes." This breakdown affects individual productivity and hinders collective efforts, leading to inefficiencies and delays in project completion.

Negativity stemming from personal conflicts and unhelpful criticism in the workplace can begin with a single poorly timed or misplaced remark. If left unaddressed, these issues can escalate, resulting in chronic stress that may cause burnout, mental health challenges, physical health issues, higher absenteeism and presenteeism, and strained team dynamics.

If you push your team to perform at unsustainable levels, employees may subconsciously interpret this as a signal that the organization undervalues their contributions and well-being, which only deepens the culture of fear. A culture of fear typically stems from poor management at some level. It could originate from a toxic manager, unrealistic expectations set by the CEO, or even board-level issues; in all cases, the repercussions are widespread. This tension often arises from authoritarian leadership styles, a lack of clear communication, punitive performance management systems, and insufficient support for employee well-being and development, or a combination of these factors. To ensure organizational survival, it is essential to address the root causes that fuel the culture of fear.

Fostering a positive, supportive, and productive workplace is a shared responsibility that everyone plays a part in, not just our leaders. It's important for team members to step in and help each other address any negativity that might arise among peers. By creating an environment where everyone feels safe to discuss these challenges, organizations can shift away from a culture of fear and naturally grow into one filled with trust, engagement, and mutual respect.

Combining compassion for staff with strategic alignment of workloads and resources creates opportunities for reducing unnecessary stress in any organization. Ignoring the issue of overburdened employees results in costs that outweigh any potential investment in supportive systems.

Wise leaders learn that doing less allows teams to accomplish more! The same rule applies to focus; without a set target, no one can ever cross a finish line or meet an obligation. Without focus, there can be no success.

If you replace fear with trust and support, you will empower your teams to innovate, collaborate, and achieve remarkable results together.

Bad Can Also Be Good (!?!)

If the source of an individual's fear can be removed, the passions that drove their bad behavior can support positive outcomes!

Negative experiences, when handled properly, can serve as powerful learning moments and catalysts for growth. While these experiences are undesirable, they do teach resilience and adaptability and illustrate opportunities for improvement.

Have you ever seen a team turn a less-than-ideal situation into a series of wins that no one could stop smiling about?

As Stanford Professor Robert I. Sutton, a professor of management science and engineering, wrote in his book, *The No Asshole Rule: Building a Civilized Workplace and Surviving One That Isn't*, any form of bullying behavior in the workplace worsens morale and productivity. In another book, GOOD BOSS, BAD BOSS: WHAT DOES THE RESEARCH SAY ABOUT LEADERSHIP? Sutton argued that even small amounts of bad behavior can decrease morale, productivity, and profitability.

Sutton believes that while his arguments might seem straightforward to most, the "no Asshole rule" is a tool we should all adopt for identifying toxic individuals and reducing abuse. He encourages us to pay attention to our feelings during interactions. The key question to ask yourself during and after an interaction is: do you feel belittled, embarrassed, or worse about yourself after meeting someone? If the answer is yes, it's worth reflecting on why, and observing whether that person generally treats those less powerful than themselves with unkindness, insults, or threats. If both your feelings and observations point to a negative pattern, then you're likely facing an "Asshole"

Sutton's analysis does allow for there to be "temporary" Assholes; People who are just having a bad day, as will happen to any of us. Recognizing that these are different from the "certified" Assholes who are "persistently nasty."

Sutton highlighted Hollywood executive Scott Rudin as a quintessential example of a certified Asshole. He noted that Rudin had dismissed 250 personal assistants - employees entirely at his mercy - over such trivial matters as receiving the wrong muffin. Sutton characterized Rudin as someone who misused his power and, rather than addressing the issues at the root of his distress and negative behavior, opted for an easier path by making others suffer the consequences of his internal conflicts.

Whenever someone prefers to inflict suffering on you rather than addressing their own pain, they are an Asshole, and you need to recognize the behavior for what it is.

When managing people, a manager will encounter a wide variety of behaviors and needs to manage them all productively and effectively. Managers can't tolerate bullies, but sometimes, we need to manage passionate individuals who lack the skills required to self-moderate and express themselves positively.

In contrast to Rudin, whom Sutton described as someone who bullied others for fun, Sutton highlighted the traits people should aspire to emulate, notably the courage to confront bullies. Not everyone has had the life experiences or training necessary to manage bullies effectively. Thankfully, this is a skill accessible to all of us, even if we haven't endured the harmful effects of bullying personally.

Intel co-founder Andy Grove was recognized by Sutton as someone who truly valued the importance of employees challenging each other's ideas and even those of their superiors. This practice is essential not just for addressing any potential conflicts, but also for ensuring that decisions are thoughtfully examined.

Thanks to Grove's initiatives, Intel empowers employees with the tools they need to engage in healthy debates and encourages new hires to participate in classes on "constructive confrontation." The program was created to teach individuals to advocate for themselves and their beliefs while knowing how to confidently address any bullies they might encounter.

An interesting, and some may initially think humorous, thought exercise for any business leader is to assess the cost of an Asshole to the company; Sutton refers to it as the Total Cost of an Asshole, (the "TCA"), to an organization.

While it is impossible to calculate the exact TCA for any organization, Sutton believed it was instructive for companies to assess how much an Asshole was costing them. Factors include the number of hours managers and HR professionals devote to the 'management' of issues caused by the Assholes' interactions with others, the cost of lost clients due to offensive behavior or actions, and the churn rate among employees from stress.

None of these are good problems, but the churn rate is particularly devastating. The loss of good people who are productive and motivated with untrained newcomers can take years to overcome.

A simple rule of thumb is that it takes six months for a new employee to become genuinely productive. Take their salary for six months and add it with the loss in productivity (comfortably use 220% of the previous employee's wages) for the same period, and you have a fair estimate of a TCA per employee. If churn becomes widespread, six months turns into years. The cost of churn to an organization as a result of stress is not cheap.

When considering their impact on churn, recall that 40% of voluntary departures are due to stress. The costs of not managing their behavioral issues add up fast.

Setbacks can become opportunities for growth if they are approached with creativity and a positive outlook.

The Intersection of Adverse Childhood Experiences and Workplace Behavior

The solution to the problems outlined by Sutton is not as simple as "no assholes allowed." Within the landscape of organizational behavior, the presence of difficult personalities, the ones that Sutton colloquially referred to as "Assholes," poses unique challenges.

An Asshole's behavior will not threaten strong leaders, as these individuals possess the capacity to assess both the Asshole and their message for its substance. They will see through the bluster and recognize if the "Asshole" is a highly productive member of the organization who needs to learn how to manage their passions appropriately.

The challenge will be to differentiate between those Assholes who can make the necessary changes to their behavior, and those who refuse.

Have you ever seen someone channel their personal challenges into incredible empathy that uplifted everyone around them?

Drawing connections between past personal traumas and workplace behavior provides us the perspective to understand how unresolved childhood issues manifests as toxic behaviors in adults.

We cannot underestimate the importance of empathy in a leader, as they need to be mindful of the frailty of the human psyche to be able to comprehend an "Asshole" as an injured individual and as a positive contributor, both separate and joined. Exploring the behaviors that result in someone being labeled an "Asshole" allows leaders to connect the dots between Adverse Childhood Experiences (ACEs) and the sometimes horrifically challenging workplace behavior of the "Assholes."

Strong leaders are not staff therapists. However, they can recognize behavioral patterns objectively and understand how to explore and develop strategies to manage most types of individual productively.

When a leader is successful in managing diverse individuals with vastly differing behaviors, they foster a healthier and more effective workplace environment for all, despite the presence of an "Asshole."

Unfortunately, some people are determined to protect themselves from hurt by presenting themselves as virtually unmanageable. We will address those characters further into this investigation.

Being an "Asshole" is not an incurable disease, but remediation does take considerable effort. The individual is an "Asshole" because of behavioral issues that reflect the mental injuries they have sustained. Their offensive behavior is indicative of the injury that remains unhealed.

Healing from any mental injury that results from abuse requires a willingness to confront what happened to them. The step is the hardest one to take and requires tremendous courage. The root issues, the injury that caused the problems to arise, are always painful. There would be no bad behavior if the individual had not been seriously injured.

For anyone to heal from abuse, they must first accept that they are injured. Admitting that the incident(s) that inflicted the injuries upon you occurred is painful and can be devastating. We tend to bury these childhood memories and avoid any opportunity to surface or examine them. It's easy to understand why; as long as they go unaddressed, they remain an open wound, inflicting pain that no one else can see.

The result of abuse is a long-term, chronic injury that cannot heal without examination. But because the damage is physically invisible, it can be horrifically difficult for anyone to accept that they are mentally injured. Just as Descartes stated, "I think therefore I am," people are who they think they are. Accepting one has been psychologically damaged is tricky as it forces an individual to question who *they really are* versus who *they believe they are* at the most fundamental level.

Fortunately, when you confront the damage that was done to you, you give yourself permission to embrace the values that represent *'who do I want to be.'* Accepting how or why you were injured is not easy, and may never be understood. Any abuse is horrific, otherwise there wouldn't be any damage. Addressing a mental injury requires incredible courage, strength, and self-awareness, and doing so is necessary if the individual hopes to find happiness.

Sadly, due to society's stigma surrounding mental health challenges, individuals often fear admitting their struggles for fear of repercussions, leading them to deny their injuries.

Consequently, it becomes unlikely that negative behaviors will change. By avoiding acknowledgment of their suffering, they feel no need for repair: "If it ain't broke, don't fix it."

A person's unwillingness to engage in self-reflection and face their challenges harms not only themselves but also those nearby. These issues extend beyond the workplace. Regrettably, their past experiences shape their reactions to various stimuli, and often they unwittingly pass on the same harm to their children or vulnerable employees, thus perpetuating a cycle of abuse that underlies many behavioral issues.

When encountering individuals that Sutton would classify as an "Asshole," it's important to understand that their behaviors indicate the likelihood they may have experienced abuse, and they haven't yet found the strength or support to confront its effects.

If you're among the fortunate ones who haven't faced abuse, that's a blessing! And if you have faced down your challenges, be proud of the strength and support you found to heal and that you did not let those awful experiences define you.

We all face struggles throughout our lives. Recognizing them in others can lead to greater compassion both for ourselves and others. No one who suffers is fortunate endure the experience. Our challenge is to break the cycle so that others don't suffer in the future.

Fortunately, any injury can be healed, and like any other injury, mental health conditions should not be viewed as chronic diseases that are untreatable and permanent.

The CDCs data indicates that 61% of people have suffered at least one Adverse Childhood Experience. As a result, we all interact with people who have been affected by mental injuries. Most people attempt to hide their suffering, and depending on how their mental injuries were addressed, everyone will have a different approach to how they deal with interpersonal interactions. Some people become kinder and more tolerant and seek to be mediators and problem-solvers, and some become apologists or enablers for other people's bad behaviors. Finally, some become "Assholes."

Sutton's books underscored how, when their behavior goes unchecked, Assholes will create a hostile work environment. Unaddressed, their behavior leads to decreased morale, productivity, and increased challenges relating to employee retention. Objectively, one would imagine that the easy solution is to remove anyone who is an "Asshole" without hesitation.

However, when considering how to address "Assholes," we should return to the learnings from the CDC / Kaiser Permanente study from 1995-1997 on Adverse Childhood Experiences (ACEs) and consider how unaddressed ACEs shape adult behaviors. In doing so, we gain tremendous wisdom on how to manage all individuals, not just the "Assholes" in professional settings. With proper perspective, we can recognize that the answer to handling every sort of people is not simply black or white. Decisions about addressing behavioral issues should never be arbitrary.

Drawing on extensive psychological research, the ACE study showed that experiences such as abuse, neglect, and household dysfunction during formative years can be linked to the development of maladaptive behaviors and poor coping mechanisms. When these behaviors are carried into adulthood and the workplace, they manifest themselves as the aggressive, overbearing, and insensitive traits associated with Sutton's definition of an "Asshole." Occasionally, they also manifest as the mirror image to the Asshole. In either case, the degree and ways the aberrant behaviors manifest and how leaders can manage people who exhibit these tendencies represent both challenges and organizational opportunities.

One of the critical findings of Sutton's research was that bad behavior is contagious. Bad behavior that goes unchecked can create a sense of normlessness, where people feel it is acceptable to break the rules. This poor sense of normalcy can't be tolerated and needs to be eliminated. For the organization to survive and recover from contagious bad behavior, management must address the issues equitably and effectively.

As managers, we must all take the time to understand how people's ACEs impact their work lives. These people are more likely to have difficulty concentrating, managing their emotions, and interacting with others. They are also more likely to take sick days, miss work, and leave their jobs due to stressful situations.

So, when evaluating an "Asshole," a manager should assess why the behavior exists and assess the message separately from the behavior. In some cases, the "Assholes" may be the organization's most passionate advocates for better performance, and their behavioral issue rests in their struggle to deliver their message.

Reading the CDC's report on ACEs is extremely helpful, when contemplating interpersonal relationships. Reflecting on the findings can help business leaders understand how to be more effective in managing anyone, whether they suffer from a mental injury or not.

Whether or not someone suffered an Adverse Childhood Experience, we all interact with friends and family who did.

Reading the report with an open mind; the ACE Study helps any leader understand the root causes of bad behavior and offer insights on managing people more effectively. When leaders or managers understand the reasons why people misbehave, they are better equipped to develop strategies to address bad behavior.

However, you cannot be an apologist for anyone else's actions. We alone are responsible for our actions. A strong leader will learn how to manage difficult people by considering abnormal behaviors from a new perspective.

Leaders can make a real difference by understanding the different types of ACEs and how they influence people's behavior. When employees feel valued and respected, they are much less likely to exhibit negative behaviors.

Sometimes, simply understanding isn't enough, and it may be necessary to address toxic situations directly. By digging deeper into the root causes of these behaviors and recognizing the effects of ACEs, leaders can cultivate a greater sense of empathy and awareness. This understanding empowers them to manage diverse personalities effectively and to create a more positive and supportive work environment, ultimately leading to higher employee productivity.

Taking the time to understand your coworkers' personal histories will help you foster empathy and connection and will help everyone create workplaces where they feel safe and can excel.

Assholes Emerging
Early Warning Signs of Messes Ahead!

We have all felt frustration at work, and at home! When a project goes awry despite our best efforts, or a teammate lets us down, or our boss oversees us poorly and fails to provide clear direction, we feel frustrated.

However, when frustration morphs into a state of continuous irritation, anxiety, or even anger, the emotion serves as a smoke alarm, signaling that something far more serious is amiss in our relationships. Just as smoldering embers can ignite a raging fire, frustrations will explode into a toxic culture if left unaddressed.

With proper attention and care, these risks can be mitigated before they erupt into full-fledged crises. The key lies in understanding the root causes of persistent frustration and restoring healthy communication channels to create positive working relationships.

Have you ever wondered how some people can transform challenging behaviors into opportunities for connection and teamwork that amazed everyone?

First, let's explore the difference between constructive discontent and damaging frustration. It's completely normal for an employee to occasionally feel dissatisfied with performance issues, inefficient processes, or organizational hiccups. This constructive discontent can actually inspire them to learn from those challenges and seek meaningful improvements. On the flip side, when their efforts to improve things hit roadblocks that dampen their spirits, that dissatisfaction can sadly turn into complacency.

Unlike constructive discontent centered on impersonal issues, this complacency is of a professional and personal nature that will quickly devolve into a sense of powerlessness. When unaddressed, an individual's frustrations will fester into resentment and sow the seeds of a toxic culture.

Frustration typically leads to feelings of helplessness, pushing individuals to internalize negativity through anxiety and self-doubt. However, some express their frustration externally through complaints and aggression, which can damage already strained relationships and hinder productivity. Unsurprisingly, studies show that teams facing regular frustration and a sense of constant blame tend to perform poorly on complex tasks that demand collaboration, creativity, or innovation.

Since flawed communication sparks and fuels frustration, dousing the flames must begin by objectively assessing and auditing communication channels to extinguish it. Leaders must gain actionable insights into the core issues behind this frustration before devising a solution. Employing a thorough discovery process enables effective identification of solutions. However, a lack of an objective system that encourages expressing concerns will result in low participation. In environments marked by complacency, those hesitant to face internal criticism or conflict often refrain from proposing changes that may disturb their peers. Acknowledging the existence of problems is merely the beginning; addressing them demands consistent effort.

It's critically important for parties to find ways to open up honest channels of communication and bring issues to light. In fact, it is the key to easing frustrations. When managers aren't aware of a problem, they can't address them. Whether they should know about the situation or not, it's crucial for the staff to help management be aware by voicing their concerns. If employees fail to speak up, they are unintentionally contributing to the ongoing problems.

If you manage a team and no one ever questions you or raises any concerns, you must ask yourself if your communication skills and systems are perfect, or if people are afraid to ask questions! When considering indifference and fear, fear is the more problematic of the issues.

Regardless of which is true, it's guaranteed that if no one ever has any questions, the staff is waving a red flag, counseling you that a communication problem exists and a storm is brewing.

I often emphasize that this situation is fundamentally binary. If people don't ask questions, it means either you are communicating magnificently, or there's a problem. While you may occasionally communicate exceptionally well and pre-emptively address any questions, even the best communicators usually will need to clarify their points. When individuals refrain from asking questions and just follow instructions, they have become, at the very least, indifferent. More likely, they may fear potential backlash for expressing concerns.

When silence takes the place of active engagement, it indicates a clear decline or complete loss of loyalty, with people's focus shifting towards the psychological safety of remaining unnoticed until they can explore new job opportunities.

When communication flows up, down, and every which way across the organization, and relationships are rooted in mutual trust and respect, frustration will never take root. However, it is inevitable that even with the best systems and intentions in place, mistakes will happen. When they do, gaps and weaknesses will emerge and affect how reliably information is shared and filtered through silos.

When mistakes happen, the vision outlined when team members joined the organization falls out of alignment with the current reality, and people feel disconnected. If efforts to remediate issues are not supported and practical coaching on improvement is absent, doubt and frustration set in.

A further example occurs when managers stop using constructive criticism to provide concrete guidance for success. No one can succeed without a measuring stick. Imagine being in a situation where you are informed that a document you produced is acceptable, but it is in the wrong voice for the intended audience. When receiving this kind of feedback, anyone would expect to also be told how to make the document great and what changes are required to adapt for the desired audience.

Without the required and desired guidance, people work in confusion and because their manager did not take the time required to communicate properly, they feel disrespected. By continuously re-assessing all f communication patterns, organizations will identify any weaknesses that breed frustration and toxicity and can target these areas for repair.

Unproductive frustration stems from ineffective communication, leading to feelings of powerlessness. Reestablishing proper communication channels enables individuals to voice their concerns in resolving issues and implementing improvements, which will swiftly empower employees and foster loyalty. Awareness and acknowledgment of the problem are essential, as is the case with any challenge.

Unfortunately, many executives fear acknowledging the situation due to their own limitations, viewing it as a sign of personal weakness. Similar to confronting personal challenges, recognizing that a problem exists is the first and crucial step towards finding a resolution.

When leaders encourage respectful discussions about plans and decisions, employees feel reassured that every viewpoint is valued. Executives who openly share the reasoning for their choices, including those they chose not to follow, can genuinely express regret for any negative effects on their team. This openness fosters transparency, enabling everyone to reflect on decisions and showcase the integrity and compassion essential for enhancing group dynamics.

Similarly, investing in opportunities for team members to appreciate the rationale behind each other's positions pays dividends. Even the most understanding people occasionally disagree.

When the disagreement involves something both parties are deeply concerned about, they sometimes need help mediating the resulting disputes.

Engaging in open and honest conversations fosters a mutual comprehension of the issues, transforming individual frustrations into opportunities for inclusive solutions. A small investment in proactive communication today can avert significant cultural challenges in the future. By viewing frustration as a cautionary signal instead of mere background noise, organizations can sidestep internal strife, ensuring that progress remains on track.

Even the most challenging personalities can be inspired to grow when they are approached with empathy, patience, and a focus on solutions.

When Frustration Crosses the Chasm
How losing control of productive dissent leads to toxicity

Imagine the feelings that emerge when an ambitious team effort fails or when an innovation proves to be more disruptive than beneficial.

When a team faces adversity without proper support, unaddressed frustration and burnout often escalate into open hostility or disengagement. Management needs to be sensitive to these frustrations and equip themselves and their teams with strategies to address these risks early, before conflicts reach critical levels.

Sometimes, missing the mark is due to factors outside anyone's control, and the failure becomes an opportunity for a lesson. However, when managers do not learn from previous errors, problems are avoidable, and repeated missteps breed discontent among team members.

Have you ever watched a colleague turn their frustration into a burst of creativity
and solve a problem no one else could crack?

While early in the cycle of errors, some frustration will be voiced by team members blowing off steam around the office water cooler, at what point does blowing off steam begin to slide into more damaging forms of conflict?

Leaders need to be highly aware of the mood within the organization, or else they will not be able to discern when disappointment ceases to spark progress and begins to sabotage morale.

Organizational psychologist Robert Sutton aptly stated, "Pounding rain can either nourish crops or erode soil based on its duration and intensity." Like pounding rain, workplace discontent erodes culture when left unaddressed.

Leaders understand the difference between productive disgruntlement and counterproductive resentment by examining the distinct drivers and dangers of constructive dissent versus toxic frustration. With deeper understanding, they can then nurture the former while intervening against the eruptions of the latter.

We should be encouraged when staff feel displeasure with underwhelming outcomes. If no displeasure is felt when there is a setback, the emotional fortitude required to overcome roadblocks has been lost. We need to embrace the stress that comes from positive frustration as it reflects a 'can do' attitude that the individual and team will overcome barriers to success.

Like background noise, any irritations should echo through organizations as people demand clear direction, and better support, so that they can perform better in the future. Managed properly, a wise leader understands the team's frustrations and recognizes that moderate discontent can stem from healthy engagement and must be recognized as evidence of staff's investment in their work. Properly channeled, it fuels growth and evolution.

Creativity thrives when perspectives intersect while tackling challenges, and innovation follows. So, just as silence is a warning, some grumbling can be a positive when it helps get issues out in the open for transparent examination and resolution. Within reason, constructive discontent serves as an indispensable catalyst for continuous improvement initiatives as more resilient teams, and generative ideas flows.

However, suppose a manager is unwilling to listen to their staff grumbles with an objective ear. Then, those grumbles will become more serious, and the resulting toxicity will grow like mold on a spoiled dairy product.

As a leader, you need to pay attention to silence, encourage grumbling, and support productive stress while stamping out negativity. Doing so never becomes truly intuitive and it always requires active attention. To excel, you must adopt a mindful approach.

If modest displeasure signals that you are dealing with engaged employees who are invested in quality outcomes and are to be encouraged, where is the Rubicon that transforms acceptable dissent into counterproductive discontent?

Often, the pivotal factor is whether dissent gets aired openly and receives a fair hearing aimed at resolution. Left unacknowledged or unaddressed, mild disgruntlement will fester into resentment if people feel ignored, unimportant, confused, or unable to influence needed changes.

When people lack a viable channel to communicate their challenges, creativity will quickly transform into criticism, and the ability of staff and management to cooperate is compromised. Rather than corporate goals being the focus, internal finger-pointing replaces working relationships, and people's fight-or-flight tendencies come to the forefront.

According to Sutton, this unresolved frustration fuels "Asshole-like" complaining, avoidance, decreased effort, excuses, hostility, and even overt sabotage. Because frustrated individuals cope through antisocial behavior, Sutton warns, "Embittered employees often evolve into counterproductive assholes."

Any unresolved frustrations will tear apart team cohesion as issues that go unaddressed without explanation will breed cynicism, and cynicism breeds toxicity. Once these types of sentiment take hold, people will stop resisting the emotional riptide of dissatisfaction, and morale and trust in every work relationship will decline along with engagement. Individuals who do not feel heard will inevitably direct their anger inward and more staff than ever will be poised to jump ship.

The result is akin to an emotional wildfire erupting from unresolved dissent. Instead of flames, we see toxicity burning through people's self-esteem, confidence, and ability to perform. The damage from the toxicity, if not correctly addressed, threatens enduring damage.

Because a modicum of discord enables growth while extreme frustration threatens destruction, leaders must learn how to distinguish between everyday friction that develops organizational resilience versus explosive emotions signaling a cultural threat.

Not all conflict is destructive, and some conflict can be productive.

The divide lies less in the substance of debates than in the spirit animating them. Discontent fueled by a hunger for excellence feels fundamentally different than bitterness rooted in perceived neglect.

While nipping every spark before it catches flame would be ideal, leaders shouldn't fret over occasional flare-ups. Fiery outbursts can be controlled to build stronger teams and succeed in unexpected ways. To succeed, leaders must intervene and lower emotional temperatures by first hearing people out, acknowledging their perspective as valid, and re-establishing channels for respectful debate around decisions.

It's rare that any single act can erase all goodwill, or answer everyone's questions or frustrations. But when people lose trust, the damage is often irretrievable.

We shall discuss this further later. The difference in how people act and react is the critical signal separating the good Assholes from the toxic individuals you need to jettison from your teams.

Unfortunately, during difficult times, certain people portray themselves as protectors of the vulnerable, donning the guise of morality. By doing this, they conceal their own flaws and harmful behaviors, frequently employing deceitful strategies to exploit the fight-or-flight responses of those who mistakenly think that this toxic person can shield them from danger or scrutiny.

Resolving the clash between the truths behind the challenges and the falsehoods propagated by harmful individuals becomes challenging until the root of the confusion, the toxic savior, is revealed. As Sutton noted, "An ounce of prevention against frustration saves a pound of culture cure later on."

Frustration can spark innovation and collaboration when we can channel it constructively toward shared goals.

Assholes Matter
They Also Prevent Messes

While some workplace conflicts benefit an organization by revealing raw yet valuable passions, toxicity, if left unchecked, can corrode morale, mental health, and productivity.

It's important to keep in mind that leaders who may have faced abuse during their youth might find certain personal confrontations a bit trickier to handle. While this doesn't excuse them from any poor behavior or from facing their challenges, it's helpful to understand that these individuals often excel in factual discussions. However, when the conversation shifts away from facts, they might struggle to respond as effectively in the moment. Since we don't always recognize the battles others are fighting, we might misinterpret their slower responses as signs of guilt, rather than realizing that everyone processes stress in their own unique way.

Have you ever observed someone tenaciously try to help challenging coworkers manage their behavior and build a workplace that's a model of respect and kindness?

When an individual is triggered by past trauma or abuse, they experience intense emotional turmoil that is complex and difficult to navigate. If their instinct isn't to lash out and hurt others, they usually need time to process their feelings. They often feel the urge to react to an unwarranted attack, but their childhood experiences lead them to believe that no one is receptive to hearing the truth.

If you find this concept difficult to understand, you're fortunate. So, let's consider a scenario. Picture yourself as a young child who has been abused. When you seek support, others dismiss your experience as imagined or, worse, tell you to feel ashamed and forget it ever happened. Victims of such abuse often internalize the blame, making it challenging to handle criticism or attacks. Because of what they've endured, they may believe that speaking up will change nothing. Consequently, they prefer to concentrate on facts and solutions, avoiding emotional aspects of conflicts that they have learned will lead to more suffering.

Unfortunately, we can only guess at the pain others feel and most people cannot recognize the tell-tale signs indicative of adverse experiences. Worse bullies seek out the pain, knowing they can leverage it to distract attention from their own mistakes.

In any dispute, people almost always take sides, and unless the conflict is managed correctly, someone will inevitably be in the wrong.

In time, as the number of disputes surrounding one individual builds, they become known as an "Asshole." Until people ask the right questions and deal with the truth, not rumors. To an outsider, it is inconceivable why anyone not guilty would tolerate the abuse. To the receiving party, it's inconceivable why no one would focus on facts.

Managing people requires leaders to deal with all sorts of issues, and no manner how carefully one builds a team, there will always be conflicts, and sometimes, someone becomes known as an Asshole.

Not all Assholes are evil people. As humorous as the word usage may appear to some, we can observe the differences by reducing the issue to its most basic terminology. Some people come to be viewed as Assholes within an organization because they are passionate about their work and the work of those around them. Their Asshole-like behavior is not about criticizing or demeaning other people.

Evil Assholes, however, are toxic individuals whose interactions are marked by personal attacks. In both cases, the individuals may bring important skills to an organization. However, while one is an overly passionate contributor who lacks emotional control or awareness, the bad Asshole who is unwilling to reform their behavior must be flushed!

As with anything in life, anyone who wants to learn can learn. Some people will progress more rapidly than others. Even the most passionate or volatile team members can learn to mollify their behavior and control their Asshole tendencies. An organization's leadership's most significant task is to manage and uplift all team members to perform at a higher level than when they joined the organization. It is no different when dealing with challenged individuals.

A leader's first imperative is to model and uphold dignity. Even when they themselves are under attack by Assholes!

By implementing respectful feedback guidelines and accountability policies, leaders gain exponentially more ingenuity and dedication over time. By modeling appropriate behaviors, they teach others to celebrate diverse thinking without tolerating demeaning behaviors.

When difficult personalities use personal attacks to bully or demean colleagues, particularly subordinate staff with limited power, leaders must act swiftly to stem contagion. Leaders must discern whether passionate outbursts are aimed to motivate colleagues' potential or only serve to undermine dignity. Some workplace barbs are intended to provoke a positive response, while others claim to be well-intended, but create uncertainty and stress.

In any organization, leaders and managers are faced with challenging personalities. However valuable these individuals' skills and drive are, their interpersonal skills or lack thereof, create conflict and bruised feelings. If these individuals become aware of the damage their behavior creates, and if they are willing to focus on facts and set aside their malignant behaviors, leaders can coach them to express themselves more constructively, and productively.

As Robert Sutton explored in his books on the workplace, toxicity severely impacts morale, retention, and performance. Dismissing toxic staff outright overlooks opportunities for exponential growth hidden within their personality clashes. With empathy and skillful feedback, leaders can unlock tremendous potential by transforming destructive tendencies into catalysts for growth.

Some friction is healthy and necessary. If lacking in personal attacks, it can illuminate pathways forward that homogeneous groups overlook and yield innovation where harmony stagnates.

However, difficult personalities who depend on personal attacks to score points are people manifesting poor behavior due to the impact of unresolved adverse childhood experiences that become embedded coping mechanisms, as revealed in the CDC-Kaiser Permanente Adverse Childhood Experiences Study. Their behaviors were learned early on to help them cope with and survive the trauma of abuse or neglect. As an adult, their actions are defense mechanisms, combatting childhood fears and creating a buffer around themselves by punishing others for any attempt at progress.

When employees join a workplace, they arrive with a toolbox filled with skills. But they also arrive bearing the effects of their childhood experiences that shape their positive and negative behavioral tendencies. Managers are rarely trained psychologists, yet they must learn the skills to manage various personalities and coach them to become their best contributors. The manager's impact, however, does not stop at the doorway to the office, as the example they set is also reflected in how staff comport themselves while away from the office.

Today's staff is tomorrow's leader, and the examples you set are ones they will emulate when leading others. Their training begins with the example a leader sets in shaping workplace culture and how they help troubled employees adopt healthier coping skills. With support, high-functioning yet provocative personalities (Assholes) can evolve from liabilities into assets, driving competitive advantages.

Despite leaving bruised feelings via blunt delivery, a redeemable "Asshole's" core aim is excellence versus ego. They refuse to accept mediocrity but are incapable of communicating high standards in ways that enlighten versus deflate. Some workplace sparks can actually signal deep care versus an aim to destroy. This distinction helps leaders recognize the capacity for growth when misconduct arises.

Even well-intended criticism that is delivered poorly will impede progress. Harvard neuroscientist Amy Arnsten explained that our brains perceive verbal assaults as physical threats. So, however vital the feedback, insensitive delivery will trigger fight-or-flight responses rather than receptivity. What began as a concern became a conflict that imperiled the project's advancement. Any feedback will be drowned if our dignity feels besieged.

London Business School's Dan Cable noted that anxiety narrows focus. Triggered employees will absorb criticism as indictments rather than guidance for improvement; anyone's receptivity will harden if there is a risk of pain.

Leaders hold the power to break this cycle by instituting guidelines that ensure respectful delivery and receipt of feedback. London and Smither's 2002 Journal of Management study confirmed that employees who perceive constructive feedback as a tool for growth, experience increased motivation and team engagement.

A positive response to feedback hinges on keeping commentary focused on behaviors rather than personal criticism. The most impactful feedback provides specific guidance toward realistic steps for progress. Failing to adhere to constructive standards will provoke self-protective reactions that boomerang and rapidly undermine group cohesion and performance. Calvin Morrill's participative management model builds on this, showing that employees who participate in decision-making will unlock exponentially more workplace vitality by engendering trust.

Emotional intelligence, which psychologist Daniel Goleman defines as "being aware that emotions drive behavior and impact people," allows leaders to discern motives underlying misconduct. Seeking first to understand rather than indict permits customizing disciplinary responses to the needs of complex personalities.

Trauma research shows that speaking truths gently and in private opens ears, while public criticism closes them and triggers emotional outbursts from irrational shame. Accountability never necessitates cruelty, and solution-focused conversations are designed to preserve dignity and prevent toxicity from mushrooming destructively.

The paradox, however, is that some dissenters who ruffle feathers also fly ahead as if summoned by curiosity to make bold inquiries. Charlan Nemeth's work confirmed that these passionate dissenters will often challenge organizational assumptions and, in doing so, spark meaningful debates that yield better solutions than cohesive groups.

Writer Esther Derby wrote that diversity and disagreement indicate psychological safety permitting risk, an incubator for innovation. From her, we discover that appropriate friction powers ingenuity.

In other words, their passions that fire the voices of dissent can be shaped into creative destruction that uncovers unexpected opportunities.

Here, history provides paradigms where impolitic voices were channeled for competitive gain.

As an example, Franklin Roosevelt famously appointed a vocal critic, Rex Tugwell to his inner circle, valuing an outsider's perspective. Tugwell's refusal to blindly endorse Roosevelt's New Deal policies led to measured compromises that bolstered consensus, leading to adoption.

Similarly, Steve Jobs embraced brutal honesty within Apple's design teams, seeing debate as essential for excellence. He instilled a culture permitting respectful challenges to authority in pursuit of exceptional products that fueled Apple's rise.

Leaders who embrace the philosophical belief that the interplay of adversity and advantage swirls with nuance display tremendous leadership savvy. They comprehend that dissent can be positive and some turbulence is required to help teams drive cutting-edge improvements.

Managing passions in individuals who lack basic self-regulatory skills can be overwhelming. Oversee people too crisply, and creativity suffers. Indulge too much incivility, and foundations erode. The solution relies on high expectations and interweaving grace throughout diverse interactions.

Transformational leadership masterfully uplifts human dignity while demanding excellence. It shows that one can be kind while keeping standards high.

Brain science confirms that reasoned appeals will eventually persuade, while force will always breed resistance. Mastering this represents one of leadership's highest craft: the skill to inspire human potential by providing a vision that guides a deeper purpose.

In the end, Assholes who are passionate about the organization's success can warn us of real problems caused by poor communications and misguided practices. To lead them, managers must learn the skills to convert the toxicity that arises from personal attacks into productive and constructive dialogue during conflict.

Recognizing and denouncing the impact of toxicity is the first step toward fostering a workplace where respect and growth are the norm.

Empathy and Managing Toxicity

Unfortunately, the lessons that we require to assist us in learning how to manage toxic individuals are not formulaic, and the number of people affected is far more widespread than we might have expected.

Have you ever worked with a leader whose empathy was so powerful it turned even the most difficult situations into opportunities for growth?

Often, many of the individuals recognized as high-performers are "Assholes" who believe that their behavior is part of their success. Of course, they cannot imagine how amazing they would become if they would adopt less toxic behaviors!

This reality underscores the importance of empathy in leadership and demonstrates how understanding the underlying causes of toxic behavior enables more effective, compassionate management.

The CDC's ACE study data indicated that 61% of adults have suffered from some form of Adverse Childhood Experience that they can identify from their childhood. Fundamentally, this means that most people have been exposed to abuse or trauma during their youth.

It's rare for anyone to know what challenges our friends and associates suffered while growing up. These are among our deepest, darkest, and certainly most painful secrets. We are only aware of what little people share, and most people are reluctant to share their stories for fear of being chastised or ridiculed.

We cannot predict or foresee who among us has unresolved issues until the moment arrives that something triggers an unexpected response from them. In fact, until the individual recognizes that their behavior is an issue, they likely will remain oblivious to the problem. This is a pain avoidance mechanism, and while undesirable, it is understandable.

When someone is triggered, people's first response is to react and mitigate the current problem, and only very rarely do we take the time to contemplate what caused an outburst.

A person who suffers from these outbursts likely has not acknowledged their root problems. This underscores the importance of empathy in leadership. Understanding the underlying causes of toxic behavior enables more effective, compassionate management. Learning the techniques required to navigate difficult situations while supporting both personal and organizational growth is a valuable, and necessary skill.

Unlike a broken arm, which anyone can see, the mental injuries that result from abuse are invisible and go untreated for many years, if ever.

When the initial injuries occurred during our childhood years, we did not know how to express our pain or explain the situation, and so we buried it within us. While a broken arm gets set in a cast, the mental injuries from the abuse or trauma that cause the injury often go untreated.

When the damage from abuse and trauma goes unaddressed, people develop a false belief that it's their fault that they were injured, and their behavior adapts. When the pain was inflicted by a parent, the child learns that they need to constantly struggle to prove themselves, and the struggle continues into adulthood.

Whether the abuser is acting intentionally or otherwise, non-physical, and emotional injuries often continue to be inflicted into adulthood. Unlike the broken arm which anyone can point to and offer sympathy, we can't see the injury. When confronted by the scars and effects on the adult's behavior, we tend to dismiss the individual as 'damaged' or an Asshole, and in doing so, we perpetrate the pain and add new damage.

Victims are not unique, unfortunately, and the impact of the toxicity is felt across generations. The injuries affect people's behavior at home and work. At home, where people feel secure enough to lower their guard and be their true selves, the abused often become the abusers, and the cycles repeat. Breaking the cycle of abuse starts at home and should be a top priority for all parents. We know that the cycles of abuse repeat. People who suffer from trauma often inflict their pain on others. Breaking that cycle starts by recognizing the behavior in oneself.

Although the roots of behavioral issues often stem from home, it is critical for business leaders to understand the impact of mental injuries on workplace behavior. By training themselves to be observant and insightful regarding these behavioral challenges, managers can learn to identify symptoms and support individuals in addressing their issues. However, it's important to note that managers are not trained mental health professionals and have limitations in their capabilities.

There exists a considerable gap between being aware of problems and being competent in addressing them. While management does not entail resolving others' mental injuries, it embodies an aspect of workplace psychology, which requires a varied skill set. To be effective, managers need to cultivate a mindful approach to conflict resolution and toxicity management through policies that minimize the potential for these issues. Additionally, by fostering 'safe spaces' in the workplace, managers enable team members to seek the support they need.

No one is perfect, and we all have blind spots. Our perspectives are shaped by our experiences and how things affect us. A manager can motivate a team to succeed by focusing everyone's attention on a list of deliverables and creating accountability through formulaic approaches. In doing so, they create boundaries and identify milestones and goals, and the resulting successes improve team members' self-esteem and willingness to push themselves further to improve.

Not all managers are leaders. Leaders intuitively work to understand people better to balance accountability and empathy when assessing and comprehending performance. They find ways to support their teams to bring accountability and success by considering their mental state.

When managers do not contemplate the psychology behind their team's behaviors, they demonstrate their inability to help maximize people's true potential. Managers with leadership capabilities will use their knowledge and experience to help others discover their potential, and support efforts to overcome any challenges. A psychological understanding of others is vital for a manager's ability to guide teams effectively, as managers will need to constantly find new ways to help individuals reduce the triggers that result in their stress (and the stress they inflict on those surrounding them) without sacrificing team performance.

Managers who aspire to be recognized as leaders and leaders who wish to become managers need to learn about the psychology of people management. These tools are indispensable in managing challenging behaviors. If a manager believes otherwise and depends on formulaic approaches, their teams will underperform because the data shows that more than half of their team is likely to be afflicted by some form of mental anguish. Ignoring that these issues exist is unacceptable and will result in lowered performance and productivity, and can result in organizational failure.

Recognizing that these issues exist and are pervasive, managers also need to be aware of their own behavior and how it affects the dynamics of everyone around them. Just because someone has become a manager should not imply they have resolved their own challenges. Managers need to be extra mindful of the behavioral examples they set, and the first step in any mindful approach centers on creating a workplace culture that emphasizes emotional intelligence and psychological safety.

Conflict at home or the workplace is inevitable, but if it can be managed constructively instead of becoming personal and destructive, then people learn and discover benefits. Sometimes, there are justifiable reasons for conflict, and when harnessed or tolerated for appropriate reasons, conflict can be productive.

Accepting that some conflict is tolerable, leaders need to foster an environment where employees feel safe to express themselves without fear of retribution, and in which behaviors that undermine their sense of safety are not tolerated. In time, we all encounter people who are less restrained or capable of controlling their emotions than we are. These people's inability to cope with the stresses of daily life reflects the unhealed injuries and poor coping mechanisms learned as a result of their ACEs.

While a passionate individual's behavioral issues may be challenging, a leader must consider why the individual is triggered, and separate their passion for quality from their deficiencies. Their positive impulses must not be discouraged, while their negative tendencies should be coached to drive them to more positive outcomes.

When dealing with an individual whose outbursts are triggered by their passion for higher quality, leaders need to deal with the behavior and evaluate what quality issue exists that requires further attention.

As leaders, we need to separate the tone of the message from the substance. This can be incredibly difficult because, when confronted with irrational outbursts, we tend to discount the messenger and do not actively listen to the message. We need to listen to the message to recognize that sometimes the "Assholes" can be 'the canary in the coal mine,' responding to what they see as a lack of effort or inattention to detail on the part of those around them.

Leaders need to determine if an individual's emotional outbursts are symptomatic of a bad character or if they reflect the individual's caring and passion for their work. In the case of caring, the "Assholes" outbursts usually reflect their frustration with their inability to motivate others to perform to their potential. A manager must differentiate between destructive tantrums and meaningful, immature demonstrations of caring and frustration.

I have dealt with a few such "Assholes" in my companies. Some I terminated outright as they were toxic individuals whose acts were beyond redemption and who exhibited no interest in reforming their behaviors. A few, however, were phenomenal contributors who wanted to improve and wanted to learn how to manage their emotions more effectively. How they responded to being challenged regarding their behavior was telling and indicative of them as people. There's no perfect solution or outcome, and change is a lifelong journey. We are all learning and making mistakes, but experience helps us avoid the same mistakes in the future!

Let's examine the case of one individual, who we will call "Joey." Joey is a highly regarded thought leader in his industry. He is dedicated to producing the finest quality products and understands that to succeed, everyone on the team must maintain the highest standards and not cut corners.

Unfortunately, Joey likely suffered from some form of trauma in his youth, and uncontrolled emotional responses often governed his adult behavior. Whenever something went awry, it only mattered that something was off, and the why wasn't immediately relevant. His responses to imperfections were emotional outbursts. But, because the outbursts always related to professional standards and personal attacks were not employed, I didn't view him in the same light, nor respond to his issues in the same way, as with another high-skilled individual (whom I dismissed) who used personal attacks to bully people.

While the other individual was terminated for being an Asshole, Joey wasn't. He was an Asshole, but he was not using personal attacks to bully people. His outbursts were highly emotional, and too often, they were excessive, but they were not personal attacks. His outbursts were his reaction to a peer or employee's substandard performance and reflected his desire to help them improve. This realization was vital in determining how to manage him and why attempts were made to support him instead of moving to immediately terminate.

Joey's skills and dedication to quality were exceptional, and his knowledge was essential for a brief time. But as extraordinary as his skills were, his interpersonal skills were equally abysmal. Despite his issues with emotional control, the team Joey worked with benefited from his passion and dedication. Tellingly, even after he left, the team continued to perform at an outstanding level.

Joey had many of good qualities that helped guide the people around him to perform to a higher standard. To his credit, he was generous in spirit and worked tirelessly with anyone who asked for his assistance. He was happy to share his knowledge freely and to teach people, and he expected the same of others. But when stressed, his lack of emotional control was horrific. It was informative that he would blow up at anyone, not just subordinates, which is atypical for a bully.

Privately, Joey admitted that he understood that his behavior was inappropriate and that he admired the ability of others to not react to adversity in the same way he did.

Unlike the "Assholes" who point fingers elsewhere, he didn't insult anyone personally, and he accepted responsibility for his mistakes. He also took full responsibility for the mistakes of anyone on his team, which showed exemplary personal leadership and fostered loyalty.

When incidents occurred, they were typically caused by his drive to perfectionism, which, as we covered earlier, is usually a reflection of poor self-esteem. Once an incident had passed and the emotional triggers were removed, he could usually explain problems and propose solutions in a calm and rational manner.

When one looks at a case like Joey, one sees a perfect example of Sutton's comment that; *"not all assholes are bad assholes!"* As counterintuitive as this may appear, Sutton advised companies to adopt the "one Asshole rule." Sutton believed that by having a couple of token jerks in a company, coworkers can observe the issues surrounding an Asshole's bad behavior and, as a result, be more likely to do the right thing, without adopting or requiring the Asshole's negativity as an unwelcome prompt.

A leader's dilemma when confronted with an ''Asshole'' is to determine whether or not their contributions can be managed to everyone's benefit.

Joey was the most difficult Asshole I've ever dealt with. All others were dispatched after warnings were ignored. As explained above, Joey was different, and I respected him for his good qualities. We sometimes disagreed on matters, but never doubted each other's commitment or desire to succeed. Even though his approach was deplorable, his passionate perspectives were informative. If he saw something a certain way and was confused, then it was clear that others who might not raise a concern would be as well.

He was a Canary in a Coal Mine. Every organization needs people who will speak up for what they believe in.

Managing individuals with strong and difficult personalities who are also phenomenally talented contributors takes a tremendous amount of effort. However, by synthesizing Sutton's hypothesis surrounding Assholes' behavioral tendencies with the concept of ACEs, a comprehensive understanding of the development of difficult personalities in the workplace emerges.

No matter what actions are taken when managing an "Asshole," their uncontrolled outbursts cannot be tolerated. If left unaddressed, the effects of their behavior will damage people and the organization. This poses a management dilemma. We need to be mindful when identifying the "Assholes," because the right "Asshole" can be an asset.

Helping an "Asshole" overcome their tendency for negative behavior takes a lot of effort via targeted intervention. To effect change, a manager must listen to passionate outbursts and respond calmly and factually to any concerns or issues. Addressing valid concerns will create trust and respect. Eventually, they will recognize the value of the modeled behavior, and gradually, modified behaviors will emerge.

Change will not occur by simply highlighting the issue and providing access to counseling or coaching, because these individuals are oblivious to how toxic their behavior is and its impact. Most of these passionate individuals will only force themselves to change when they realize the adverse effects of their behavior on productivity and the negative impact on the results they are passionate about!

In other words, they will only attempt to change when they recognize that their behavior is doing more damage than good.

Recalling that "a spoonful of sugar makes the medicine go down" can assist us in teaching improved behavior. When individuals facing difficulties realize how their struggles affect others, their drive for excellence may inspire them to embrace the behaviors necessary to achieve their goals. However, unless they choose to address the underlying issues of their challenges, these attempts remain merely temporary fixes, allowing them to function better. Their natural volatility will still simmer beneath the surface.

As a leader, it is rewarding (and a relief) to see positive behavior patterns adopted and modeled. However, these changes never happen overnight, and patience must be part of the equation.

Taking a proactive and supportive stance is much more effective in the long term than punitive measures when it comes to helping challenging team members cultivate healthier coping mechanisms and interpersonal skills. This approach also establishes a positive atmosphere for the entire team. It's essential for your team to feel that you value every individual, ensuring that even the more difficult members are treated with respect.

The role of leadership is to set the tone and lead by example. An organization's leaders and managers must always model correct behavior, especially when placing the organization's interests ahead of their own.

I have dealt with managers who proved they were not leaders through bad behavior. They were Assholes, and they were dismissed when they refused to remediate their behavior. It's simple really, if management spreads negativity or adopts the usage of personal attacks, they need to be terminated.

An employee who is emotional but does not make personal attacks is operating from a desire to help those around them succeed. A manager whose work is exemplary but whose criticisms become personal attacks must be dismissed.

People are complicated, and leading them is not for the faint of heart. No matter what you do, sometimes you can't help someone, and sometimes the people you have supported will turn on you. People find solace when they seek easy answers. They also believe it is less painful to avoid challenging their traumas rather than taking the hard steps to accountability with others. People can help themselves, but some are too scared and prefer to hide in the dark areas of their minds, attacking others to avoid confronting their own reality.

Unfortunately, while some will seek to hide, others will portray themselves as saviors, and these are the most dangerous individuals in any organization.

Empathy is the key to unlocking a team's potential by transforming conflict into connection and building a culture of mutual support.

Beware the Toxic Savior

Complex behavior that undermines organizational health

Few phenomena breed as much confusion and discord as toxic individuals proclaiming themselves to be the champions of the vulnerable in order to conceal their own machinations and divisiveness.

Like wolves hiding beneath wool coats, their selfish motives stay cleverly hidden under cloaks of righteousness woven from the fibers of the moral high ground they pretend to occupy.

Have you ever worked with someone who offered the best advice in hindsight and always knew how to "fix everything?"

These individuals are more interested in 'being right' than 'doing right.' As such, they twist fiction into 'fact' to sensationalize and evoke emotional responses, usually to portray themselves as victims while claiming to defend others. In seeking to 'be right,' their self-aggrandizing tactics undercut and fracture teams. Instead of protecting anyone, their actions disrupt focus, and the damage done turns stakeholders into victims. The true aim of their grandstanding is not to support others but to hide personal failures beneath capes of self-proclaimed virtue.

Through masterful manipulation, workplace "saviors" seduce followers into believing their behavior serves principled ends. Sadly, even the most theatrical and outlandish falsehoods will captivate audiences who seek simple explanations for complicated problems. As lies are simple to tell, this form of duplicity spreads and lingers.

Although the causes may differ, individuals who experienced bullying in their youth might feel compelled to position themselves as defenders of the workforce. They don't aim to be harmful, but their unresolved issues can impair their perspective, leading them to overreact and deflect responsibility for their mistakes. Their fear of criticism or accountability for shortcomings drives them to engage in finger-pointing and unfounded accusations, which serve not as a defense but as a way to evade uncomfortable realities. When eventually exposed, they often respond with self-righteous denials.

Narcissists are incredibly skilled at this manipulative behavior. Where a premise of this discourse is that some Assholes are good within an organization, it should be noted that no narcissists can ever be depended upon to act in the interests of anyone other than themselves.

The worst narcissists in any organization seek recognition without the desire to invest the necessary effort in success. They revel in others' achievements while constructing intricate facades of grandeur to protect their vulnerable egos.

When issues arise, rather than contribute to solution-building, they position themselves as "the voice of the suppressed," subtly leveraging toxic messaging to maintain or improve their position while feeding their ravenous and misguided sense of self-importance.

The narcissist's best allies are the poor performers within the organization who feed the narcissist's needs and camouflage their own incompetence by redirecting scrutiny toward the more responsible using the proverbial smoke and mirrors of obfuscation.

When exposed, these toxic saviors sacrifice their supporters to protect themselves or preserve their own interests. In doing so, they continue to inflict abuse and damage on the organization.

Managers and leaders should recognize toxic individuals before problems arise. These individuals often appear to be the most gregarious and engaging of individuals. Listen carefully to their words and be cautious of anyone who showcases a façade of righteousness, as this often masks the toxicity they bring. It can be easy to overlook these warning signs because we tend to focus on the best traits in others and enjoy the company of charming and entertaining people. As a result, their shortcomings may not be evident to us right away.

While no archetype uniformly categorizes the toxicity behind false saviorhood, several hallmark signs of toxic sanctimony offer signals we all need to avoid. Those cloaking self-interest in moral outrage often:

- Inflate credentials to exaggerate expertise on ethics, fairness, diversity, or defending vulnerable groups.

- Leverage emotion by framing respectful dissent as attacks on marginalized people.

- Use hyperbolic language portraying differences of opinion as earth-shattering crises.

- Peddle conspiracy theories of systemic oppression targeting those who disagree with them.

- Position themself as the lone voice of truth and conscience combatting indifference or corruption.

- Berate leadership's commitment to equity when they are held accountable for their own poor performance.

- Gossip about alleged wrongs to deflect attention from themselves.

- Exaggerate mistakes or miscommunications by others to support their ostentatious claims.

- Solicit grievances to create confusion and seek personal advantage.

This type of behavior often stems from a lack of integrity rather than high standards. When these individuals are given free rein, they tend to conceal their personal shortcomings and selfishness, presenting a polished facade of righteousness instead.

If left unaddressed, self-righteous toxicity can leapfrog through an organization in many harmful ways. Operating in the shadows, the offender's exaggerated anger often creates confusion, leading to the truth being undermined or disregarded as inconvenient.

People often favor straightforward solutions, and blaming others provides a simple way for wrongdoers to exploit the resulting confusion. This behavior ultimately harms the whole organization, and even after their accusations are proven false, the mistrust created by their negative influence frequently remains.

Organizational health suffers whenever individuals claim ethical superiority to conceal personal deficiencies.

By situating themselves as "do-gooders," toxic saviors divide people between absolutes like "allies" and "oppressors" with no middle ground available. These manufactured divisions pressure weak and impressionable individuals to flee the conflict, shattering team cohesion.

Unlike a toxic savior, a strong leader acts with integrity and focuses on purpose rather than image. The organization's survival is foremost in the leader's mind, as people's livelihoods depend on their actions. A leader who puts their team first is emotionally exposed and feels more pain from false accusations than others would imagine.

While calmly insisting on facts and proof typically exposes anyone's wild inferences as fiction, sometimes the truth is not enough. When truth becomes a commodity, facts lose their ability to convince. When too many resources are spent debating falsehoods, teams become divided into tribes claiming ethical supremacy, and everyone loses.

In summation, an Asshole who is also a narcissist can be counted upon to wreak damage to an organization just like a spoiled child whenever they are denied an unreasonable request.

When assessing any conflict, an objective observer should ask: who benefits from the conflict and what purpose does it serve? Whenever someone speaks to me about issues surrounding toxicity in their workplace, I wonder about their role in the toxicity.

True leadership balances the desire to help with the wisdom needed to empower others. It nurtures growth, encourages independence, and promotes a sense of shared accountability.

The Ripple Effect of Poorly Delivered Criticism

As noted earlier, poorly delivered criticism will have a ripple effect throughout a team. When one employee is criticized harshly or demeaningly, it creates a climate of fear and distrust within the team. This will lead to other employees withdrawing from each other and becoming less supportive of each other.

Have you observed how a tense moment can be defused by one thoughtful comment, setting off a chain reaction of positivity?

or

Have you observed a thoughtless comment start a chain reaction that resulted in bitter disputes and long-standing antipathy?

Sadly, both are easy scenarios to envisage, and the latter is easier to have happen.

Poorly delivered criticism also leads to employees becoming more critical of each other. When employees see that their manager is willing to publicly and demeaningly criticize them, they feel justified in doing the same to their colleagues. This creates a vicious cycle of criticism and negativity within the team.

Criticism is an inevitable part of any workplace and a natural part of life. We all receive criticism at some point, whether from our parents, friends, teachers, or bosses. However, criticism can be challenging to hear and accept, especially when it is not correctly delivered.

That poorly delivered criticism will have a ripple effect within a team has been well-documented in organizational psychology.

When an employee is subjected to harsh or demeaning criticism, it doesn't just affect the individual; it sends shockwaves through the entire team. A study by Porath and Pearson in the Harvard Business Review (2013) on "The Price of Incivility" illustrates this impact vividly. They found that employees who were on the receiving end of incivility had a diminished work effort, quality of work, and time spent at work. Moreover, the witnesses to such behavior also reported a significant decrease in performance and engagement.

The negative ripple effect fosters an environment of fear and distrust within the team. If allowed to persist, this atmosphere can result in a situation where mistakes or shortcomings are concealed instead of being openly discussed due to fear of punishment. This apprehension hinders creativity and innovation, as team members become reluctant to take risks or suggest new ideas. Research by Farh and Chen (2014) in the Academy of Management Journal indicated that negative feedback often triggers defensive responses instead of encouraging constructive change when seen as a threat.

Moreover, the impact of poorly delivered criticism on team dynamics can be profound. Team members may start withdrawing from one another, becoming less communicative and cooperative. This withdrawal can lead to a breakdown in the supportive relationships essential for effective teamwork. Research by Felps, Mitchell, and Byington (2006) in the Journal of Applied Psychology found that negative behavior like incivility and disrespect can decrease group cohesion and collective efficacy.

This analysis has significant implications, reinforcing the belief that teams marked by fear, mistrust, and inadequate support struggle with productivity, innovation, and responsiveness to challenges. Employees in these environments are more susceptible to stress and burnout, which contributes to elevated absenteeism and turnover rates. A study by Bakker and Demerouti (2007) published in the Journal of Managerial Psychology revealed that workplaces with poor interpersonal relationships and detrimental feedback practices experience higher burnout rates and reduced job satisfaction. Such a toxic culture can create a domino effect, influencing not only the team but also the larger organization, as highlighted by Molinsky and Margolis in the Harvard Business Review (2005).

It is crucial to approach any conversation with a positive and supportive attitude. If you start with negatives, an individual's defensive responses will most likely prevent them from accepting your input. For this reason, managers also need to be specific and objective in their feedback.

Generalizations are useless, and any comments that are or are interpreted as personal will come across as confrontational and personal attacks.

Managers need to understand that feedback and constructive criticism do not occur in a vacuum and are not limited to review sessions. The positive elements and support of feedback need to be continuous to be practical. When delivered effectively, constructive criticism can help employees identify areas for improvement and grow and develop. However, poorly delivered criticism can devastate employee morale, team cohesion, and productivity.

The ripple effect of criticism that isn't delivered well extends beyond just creating a challenging atmosphere in the workplace. It also reaches our customers and clients, who can sense the emotions of the team. When employees feel demoralized and mistrustful, they may struggle to stay engaged in their work and might not provide the outstanding service we all aim for.

When managers single out an employee for criticism, it fosters a climate of fear and distrust within the team. Conversely, constructive support is equally contagious! In a positive environment, individuals actively seek out constructive feedback, which helps prevent employees from isolating themselves and becoming disengaged.

Poorly delivered criticism will usually have a ripple effect throughout a team:

> - Employees who are afraid of being criticized are less likely to share their ideas and collaborate with each other. This leads to a decrease in innovation and creativity.
>
> - Employees who are unhappy with their work environment are likely to leave their jobs. This can lead to increased turnover costs and disruption to the team.
>
> - Employees who are demoralized and distrustful are less likely to be productive. This can lead to missed deadlines and decreased profitability.

Team morale and cohesion are essential for any team's success. When team members trust and respect each other, they are more likely to work together effectively and achieve their goals. However, when team members feel constantly criticized, they are less likely to feel engaged in their work and more likely to feel anxious and stressed.

Team members who believe they cannot trust each other to be supportive and constructive, are less likely to communicate effectively. This makes it difficult for the team to achieve its goals and leads to a more toxic work environment, a decrease in productivity, and an increase in turnover.

Thoughtful feedback has the power to inspire change and uplift teams, creating a ripple effect of growth and positivity.

Exiting Toxic Business Relationships

Toxicity isn't just about interpersonal issues; it can show up in so many subtle ways that will affect an organization. If left unaddressed, these feelings can become ingrained within a company culture. I once worked with a client who experienced just that. Their established systems and processes ended up fostering an "us vs. them" mindset, where fear of not fitting in overshadowed collaboration and trust.

When an organization becomes overly focused on strict processes, it can create toxic relationships with any entities that deviate from these norms. In such cases, both parties must evaluate the situation to understand what occurred and how to adapt in the future. Some organizations might choose to conform and endure the toxicity, while others may decide to end the partnership. However, conforming is not the ideal choice; it's similar to staying in a loveless marriage where only a bare existence remains. Some individuals may choose to stay due to a sense of obligation, while others may opt to leave.

> *Have you ever seen someone walk away from a toxic situation with grace and clarity, teaching others about the value of self-respect?*

People often remain in relationships longer than necessary, and looking back, we can see why we should have left earlier. While hindsight may be skewed, it serves as a valuable learning tool. For instance, a few years prior to Covid-19, I supported a group engaged in a major project. Unfortunately, this project turned out to be a poor fit between the client and the service provider. To maintain confidentiality and because there are no grievances to address, I've changed the names of the parties involved. The group I aided will be referred to as "Stellar Solutions."

Stellar Solutions was an ad hoc group composed of top marketing experts who came together to complete a project. The leadership team members were internationally recognized for their expertise and innovative marketing strategies. They were high achievers accustomed to earning substantial incomes from campaign ROI. However, they encountered a major challenge while collaborating with a government infrastructure development agency (the "Agency").

The Agency's leadership had enlisted Stellar to bring creativity and vitality to its outdated and ineffective initiatives. Their request for dynamism aligned perfectly with Stellar's expertise in creating memorable and impactful marketing strategies.

Initially, the teams collaborated to pinpoint several areas ripe for enhancement. Following a review of the client's past performance, Stellar recommended strategies and innovative initiatives aimed at optimizing processes and facilitating swift success testing. These recommendations promised significant cost reductions during implementation and ensured lasting, memorable results. Upon evaluating the analysis, the Agency's leadership expressed their endorsement of Stellar's suggestions. Both Stellar and the agency's leaders shared enthusiasm in executing the strategies and eagerly anticipated the beneficial transformation they would foster.

As the Stellar Solutions team moved into the implementation phase, they faced a major challenge: the entrenched bureaucracy of the Agency. Each proposal encountered significant resistance due to extensive paperwork, delays, compliance checks, and protracted approval processes. Even simple changes demanded a tiring array of forms, reports, and reviews, compounded by middle managers who were protective of their domains and resistant to change. When confronted with data-driven insights for action, middle management prioritized reasons for postponement or inaction instead of making decisions.

The staff clearly found any change intimidating, and it quickly became apparent that their performance review criteria did not account for ROI from initiatives. In contrast, management was evaluated based on the ROI of their activities. This set up an unrealistic and unmanageable situation. To complicate things further, each member of the Agency developed an operational silo around their role, shielding themselves from scrutiny, which they perceived as a form of protection accountability.

Stellar's team of creatives and innovators were disheartened by the frustrating delays caused by Agency staff. They found it challenging to maneuver through the complicated processes, and it often felt like time and resources were slipping away. With their work intrinsically tied to their earnings, every wasted moment had a direct impact. Unfortunately, this compounded their difficulties, as their limited ability to act meant they were missing out on that rewarding feeling of accomplishment success.

The Stellar team felt a growing sense of frustration as they saw valuable opportunities for success hindered by the client's hesitation with paperwork and their reluctance to embrace new ideas. Even though they had the expertise, strong support from the Agency's leadership, and persuasive arguments, the ingrained bureaucratic culture and strict regulations made it quite challenging to bring about the important changes that were desperately needed.

Stellar's team was faced with a conundrum. Despite possessing the skills and solutions to enhance the client's operations, the bureaucracy made it challenging to make any real progress. This inability to move forward left the team feeling frustrated, and they worked hard to keep any negativity from affecting their morale. Rather than focusing on boosting performance, they found themselves preoccupied with paperwork and counting down to the contract's end date. The idea of renewing the contract seemed less exciting than it should have been.

In the end, both the client and Stellar were unwilling to pursue the collaboration further. As outsiders, Stellar struggled to assist the hesitant middle managers in overcoming their apprehensions, and their efforts for support were met with resistance. Nonetheless, as a private company dedicated to delivering results and maximizing profits for both themselves and their clients, the Stellar team gauged their success by their influence and income. Their ability to generate reasonable revenue depended on their activities, and an emphasis on paperwork significantly reduced their earning potential.

So, while the Agency's staff wanted to focus on paperwork to preserve their incomes, the focus on pedantic paperwork undercut Stellar's ability to make an impact and earn a market-rate income from the project.

Ultimately, the partnership between the consulting firm and the government agency came to an end. In retrospect, it's evident that the Agency's internal issues needed resolution prior to the engagement. Nevertheless, discussions with Agency leadership revealed that management's dissatisfaction with their own personnel greatly outweighed that of Stellar's.

Everyone had entered the initiative with positive intentions. Yet, as they faced the realities of change, a fearful workplace atmosphere began to overshadow those hopes. On one hand, the organization welcomed new and energetic leaders eager to bring about the changes needed for better outcomes. On the other hand, they encountered a seasoned staff that, familiar with the agency's employment policies, felt secure in their positions, believing they were shielded from accountability as long as they kept up with their documentation.

It was ironic. A system designed to ensure people know what to do in their roles had become so restrictive that it rendered efforts to succeed through innovation impossible.

Fortunately, success is never achieved by a failure to attempt. It is through failure that we discover ways to succeed and drive success.

The client's leadership recognized their frustrations with the staff privately. However, because of the staff's employment agreements, they lacked the authority to mandate that the staff implement the changes the board wished to see. This capitulation to existing bureaucracy highlighted the complexities and challenges involved in initiating change within institutions that are hesitant and resistant to straying from established norms.

What was clear was that despite leadership's desire for progress, successful changes would only be attainable with the support of the staff, which was being systematically withheld. No organization that refuses to change will ever succeed. Any adherence to the traditional "it's how we do it" process must be the first casualty for any successful change.

The challenges faced by Stellar are typical of, yet not limited to, government agencies. Recognizing that significant change in any organization cannot be effectively mandated from the top without buy-in across all levels is crucial. For change to succeed, leaders need to engage with their teams actively, sharing the vision and the advantages that the changes will entail.

To successfully implement change, even the ones related to improving communications systems to reduce stress, it's crucial to recognize and tackle the underlying reasons for resistance before introducing new initiatives. Resistance often arises from fears related to job security, the unknown, and failure. As leaders, we must foster a supportive environment where our teams can voice their concerns and collaborate on solutions. This might include offering extra training and support, assuring employees that their input is important, and celebrating successes.

No organization that refuses to change can ever succeed. Adherence to the traditional "it's how we do it" process must be the first casualty of any attempt at improvement.

Leaving toxicity behind opens the door to opportunity, growth, and a renewed focus on what truly matters.

Leave People Better than You Found Them

Your mission as a peer, manager, parent, or a partner should be to empower individuals, leaving them stronger and more capable than when you first encountered them. Whether your interaction lasts for a brief moment or a lifetime, your influence should be significant.

The optimal leadership mindset aims to support and uplift others, even when faced with challenging interactions. To be successful as leaders, we must advocate for compassionate, growth-oriented approaches to feedback and relationships and constantly work to ensure that everyone is positively impacted by their workplace experiences.

> *Imagine what it's like to work with someone whose words and actions are so sincerely positive that being around them makes you feel inspired and motivated to be your best self.*

When delivered and received respectfully, constructive criticism unlocks abundant human potential. Conversely, poorly handled feedback impedes performance, stifles innovation, and erodes morale. As Google learned through painful public scandals, unresolved toxicity depresses engagement while fueling attrition, and the resulting animosity compromises competitive advantage.

With committed leadership, even the most challenging personalities can be retrained from detractors into drivers of excellence. This organizational cultural engineering relies on guidelines and accountability to ensure dignified interactions. Training in emotional intelligence further orients groups towards growth and celebrates diverse thinking without accepting demeaning actions. Masterful leadership artfully transforms friction into fuel, propelling teams to heights that homogeneity inhibits.

Instituting organization-wide policies for respectful engagement, which is critical for success, requires that any commentary on mistakes and failures focus on specific behaviors rather than personal attacks and that feedback outlines realistic next steps for improvement.

Without effective guidance and delivery, criticism often leads to defensive reactions instead of openness. By equipping staff with appropriate training, a foundation for teams to handle conflicts with empathy is created. For success in this and all other processes, leaders need to demonstrate vulnerability and be open about their limitations while encouraging honest feedback and truthfulness. Emotional intelligence calls for an effort to comprehend the intricate motives behind behaviors before we respond.

When properly armed with the skills we've developed to enhance clarity in feedback, managers can become highly effective at engineering the corporate culture. These skills channel passionate communication into constructive pathways without diminishing enthusiasm. Research on mindfulness indicates that taking critical feedback less personally contributes to a greater sense of wholeness.

Problematic behaviors commonly stem from positive intentions mixed with awkward expression. A manager who thoughtfully explores the reasons behind incidents can achieve more lasting value and long-term behavioral improvements compared to those who instinctively impose penalties for errors. Even disruptive approaches can constructively question assumptions if inquiries are rooted in recognition of talent prior to discussing performance issues. Assuming negative intent and quickly resorting to punitive measures will likely lead to repeated behaviors.

By demonstrating grace under pressure, leaders will elicit exponentially more support, ingenuity, and dedication from team members. We all stumble and get knocked down at times. Sometimes, it takes people more time to recover, regroup, and rise again. Despite setbacks, the desire within leaders to help those around them achieve their potential and do great things is never extinguished.

Leaders today are tasked with embodying the change they aspire to create. Individuals embrace organizational values by witnessing them honored in everyday actions that correspond with key priorities. Essentially, leaders function like choirmasters, harmonizing diverse voices to achieve common objectives, and their effectiveness is crucial for fostering the creativity and unity needed to remain competitive.

This showcases the beautiful artistry of nurturing our human gifts, even in the midst of workplace conflicts. True leadership understands that serving people and enhancing performance go hand in hand. When we uplift dignity, we can truly unlock the potential within each person.

As stated at the outset, being constructive and respectful is easy, so why do we need to expose constructive criticism as a business communication challenge? The answer is simple: humans are complicated creatures. We will only be encouraged to improve if we are reminded of our weaknesses and offered reasons to improve.

Any transformative journey begins with modeling the behaviors you wish to see developed in yourself. As you rise through an organization's ranks, prioritize open dialogue around conflicts, viewing them as opportunities for collective learning rather than grounds for punishment. When addressing misconduct, seek to understand the underlying causes before determining consequences.

Keep in mind that leadership focuses on progress rather than perfection. You will encounter setbacks and obstacles throughout your journey. What truly matters is your response. Strive to exemplify humility, curiosity, and an unwavering dedication to growth. By regularly aligning your actions with your values, you'll motivate others to do the same.

Ultimately, your legacy as a leader will be measured not by short-term gains but by the impact on the lives of those you touch.

Creating a culture of constructive feedback allows everyone to thrive and helps build a more compassionate and innovative world. Embrace the exciting challenge of this transformative journey with courage and belief in yourself. Remember, every small step taken towards enriching your feedback culture is a valuable addition to enhancing your team, your company, and our society. Though the path ahead might seem lengthy, the personal and professional rewards along the way are immeasurable.

By demonstrating high standards under pressure, leaders elicit more ingenuity and dedication from team members. Leaders are human, and we all stumble. However, our desire to help those around us is never extinguished.

Authentic leadership recognizes no separation between the service of people and the service of performance.

As leaders, the greatest impact we can have is to uplift others, leaving them stronger, more confident, and ready to succeed.

Delivering Criticism Constructively and Effectively

Using a carrot and stick strategy, scolding, or even resorting to a whip might have been seen as acceptable for boosting productivity in the past, yet bullying and abuse have never been effective methods for enhancing performance. We have always recognized this, but ineffective leaders opted for easier ways to cling to their positions within a hierarchical, top-down management structure.

Fortunately, managers today have positive and constructive alternatives for delivering criticism effectively. This approach is essential for fostering strong organizations. By presenting criticism as a chance for growth and emphasizing clarity, empathy, and respect, a foundation for continuous improvement is established improvement.

As we each explore the development of our unique styles, let's remember that learning from our mistakes is a valuable part of the journey! Everyone makes errors, and that's perfectly normal; what matters is that we continue to grow and embrace the learning process. Even when we encounter challenging situations, there's always room for growth from those experiences and the lessons they bring.

However, despite the best intentions of any management team, negative behaviors and practices can still pop up in organizations. But by keeping open lines of communication and feedback, we can catch issues early and prevent negativity from taking root. Together, we can create a healthier and more supportive environment for everyone! Acting properly is not hard. The rules are easy to follow, and they mimic what you should expect to experience in every relationship, at work, and at home:

- *Be timely.* Give feedback as soon as possible after the event occurs. This will help employees understand the impact of their behavior and make necessary changes. It is also essential to give feedback promptly so the employee can learn from their mistakes and move on.

- *Be private.* Give feedback in a private setting. This will help the employee to feel more comfortable and to be more open to receiving feedback.

- Be respectful. Be mindful of your tone of voice and body language. Avoid being condescending or accusatory. Focus on the behavior, not the person. When giving feedback, focus on employee behavior, not personality. Be clear on this.

- Be supportive. Even if you must deliver a reprimand or negative feedback, respecting and supporting the employee is essential. Remember that everyone makes mistakes, and feedback should aim to help the employee improve.

- Be willing to listen to feedback. When giving feedback, be open to hearing the employee's perspective. Remember that feedback is a two-way street. You learn about people's needs and concerns by listening to people's feedback.

- Be constructive. When giving feedback, focus on the specific behavior or outcome that needs to be improved.

- Be specific about a mistake and why it is a problem. Avoid using vague or judgmental language, personal attacks, or general statements.

- Focus on the future. Once you have given feedback, focus on helping the employee to improve their performance. Offer to provide support and resources.

By following these basic rules, any manager can deliver constructive criticism in a helpful and supportive way, and adhering to these policies will create a more positive and productive work environment.

Communication is fundamental to success. Based on your experiences, you should intuitively understand how poorly delivered or managed feedback can negatively impact productivity.

Companies need to act decisively when introducing new systems aimed at equipping managers with the skills to provide effective criticism. Implementation of these systems is not a one-time event; businesses seeking to enhance and uphold their corporate culture recognize that it's an ongoing process for employees to feel at ease receiving feedback and responding positively.

Happier employees have higher self-esteem and know they are valued, and they transmit those beliefs to the people around them, benefiting everyone! A more positive and productive work environment means people go home happy. People who go home from work stressed and in a foul mood take their pain with them and inflict it on their families.

Break the cycle, and recognize what truly matters.

Constructive feedback is a gift that empowers others to grow. Properly delivered also it teaches others how to foster a culture of trust and continuous improvement.

The ONE Chapter

If you need to break the glass, start here

If you only read one chapter in this book, this is the one you need the most!

This book was written as a collection of articles. While each chapter can be read as a stand-alone to provide insights and perspective, some people are in periods of crisis at work and need quick guidance. They need immediate help, and that's why I wrote this chapter. It's "The ONE Chapter you need to read."

Managing difficult personalities at work can be a bit tricky, but with a thoughtful approach, we can turn those tough situations around! Inspired by insights that appear throughout the book, this article shares practical strategies to effectively deal with problematic behavior, promote a culture of respect, and keep our workplaces uplifting and productive for everyone.

The first step in managing challenging personalities is to create clear expectations for behavior and communication. While many organizations believe their employees grasp workplace norms, it's easy for misunderstandings to arise without clarity, which can allow interruptions to become accepted.

Dealing with strong, difficult personalities who are also highly talented requires significant effort. Yet, by integrating Robert Sutton's insights on "Assholes" behavior with the concept of Adverse Childhood Experiences (ACEs), managers can gain deep insights into effectively managing challenging personalities in the workplace.

Regardless of the strategies used to handle "Assholes," failing to address their undesirable behaviors will harm the organization. While managing "Assholes" presents significant challenges for managers, doing so successfully offers tremendous benefits. Be careful judging these individuals, as the right "Asshole" is often among the most invaluable assets to the organization.

A vital component of leading staff will be in how they assess you and your efforts to manage the most difficult of your peers and staff. Everyone, no matter how unpopular they may be, needs to be treated equitably and fairly. Your job is to ensure that this occurs. While "Assholes" will take longer and be more difficult to remediate, the premise of constructivism in the workplace demands that progress be supported, and empathy be applied to accept the flaws and judge efforts at improvement fairly.

Leaders can create a positive atmosphere by clearly defining acceptable behaviors in their policies, during training sessions, and through ongoing discussions with teams. Most importantly, they must exemplify the behavior they wish to see in others. By illustrating expectations regarding respect, accountability, and constructive feedback, confusion can be reduced, and a strong cultural foundation established. This approach ensures that everyone understands and respects the organization's values.

An essential next step is nurturing leaders to skillfully handle challenging personalities by giving them the tools and awareness they will need to deal with sensitive situations. Successfully managing toxic behavior involves a thoughtful approach, including de-escalation techniques and emotional intelligence training.

Equipping managers with skills in constructive communication allows them to gently guide difficult employees toward greater self-awareness and accountability for their actions. Engaging in role-playing scenarios with team leaders can boost their confidence and proficiency in tackling disruptive behavior when it arises. Emotional intelligence training stands out here, empowering leaders to navigate tough interactions with empathy and understanding, which can ease tensions and lower defensiveness during challenging times.

An effective approach for managing toxic personalities is to give feedback constructively and clearly. When dealing with a challenging employee, focus on specific behaviors rather than vague personality traits. General remarks like "You have a bad attitude" can alienate employees and lack useful direction. Instead, offer feedback that targets specific actions. For instance, saying, "During yesterday's meeting, you interrupted your colleagues multiple times," makes the criticism easier to accept and points out potential improvements.

Presenting feedback as a chance for growth rather than a punishment can help transform the employee's view, motivating them to see the advice as a pathway to professional development and growth.

For leaders managing difficult personalities, maintaining consistency and follow-through is crucial. When a disruptive employee ignores or disregards feedback, it often becomes necessary to progressively implement more severe corrective measures to reinforce that standards will be upheld. This process may start with informal coaching and progress to formal feedback sessions.

If formal feedback sessions do not yield results, the employee should understand that a failure to make meaningful attempts to improve their behavior will ultimately result in termination. The goal is to avoid punishment and instead make it clear that the organization prioritizes positive and productive interactions. At every stage, we must avoid communicating a "do this or you're out" mentality, as such a strategy is inherently toxic. If a lack of improvement does result in termination, the impacted team member will recognize that they were treated fairly, and it was their choices that resulted in this outcome.

Consistency is crucial in people management, as it helps mitigate perceptions of favoritism or bias. It demonstrates that all team members are held to equivalent standards. However, this gets complicated when handling a star performer, as other colleagues may subconsciously perceive preferential treatment. The manager's challenge is to ensure steady leadership, providing all staff with fair and equal treatment. Advancement from any employee must be recognized as progress. While some may progress more slowly than others, it's essential to distinguish the sincerity of their efforts.

Keeping communication channels open is essential for effectively managing challenging employees! Leaders can create thoughtful opportunities, such as regular check-ins, anonymous feedback options, and confidential counseling services, where team members can comfortably share their thoughts on toxic behaviors without fear of backlash. This friendly approach not only allows leaders to catch potential issues early but also ensures that everyone's concerns are recognized and truly valued. By providing a safe, judgment-free space for employees to discuss workplace dynamics, we nurture increased awareness and empathy within the team. When employees feel heard, they're more likely to engage in positive discussions and collaborate on solutions, which helps prevent frustrations with difficult coworkers from piling up

Effectively managing difficult personalities often necessitates a deeper understanding of the root causes behind their behavior. Their issues may arise from personal insecurities, past negative experiences, or mental health struggles. Here, empathy and understanding from leadership can turn a challenging situation into a chance for growth. Leaders who adopt a personalized approach by recognizing the employee's strengths and weaknesses are more likely to help them address their challenges. Engaging in one-on-one discussions in a supportive, nonjudgmental setting can reveal underlying issues the employee faces and explain their behavior. While this method doesn't justify anyones destructive actions, it helps to humanize the individual and creates a setting conducive to change.

Another effective approach involves fostering self-reflection and accountability among employees. Encouraging challenging individuals to participate in self-assessment activities, such as reflecting on their communication styles or taking personality tests, can help them identify patterns in their behavior. Many companies utilize tools such as the Myers-Briggs Type Indicator (MBTI) or the Enneagram to provide employees with insights into both their own behavior and that of their peers. By collecting this data and then offering resources and training tailored to an individual's personality type, managers can help their employees adjust their approaches and create healthier interactions with coworkers.

Leaders need to approach collaboration strategically, particularly when working with challenging personalities in structured group settings. When done effectively, group collaboration demonstrates healthy interpersonal interactions to difficult individuals. Although they may struggle to adjust their own skills independently, these experiences provide relatable examples that contribute to their self-reflection. Discussions about their experiences will help cultivate their positive behaviors. Assigning roles that utilize their strengths while holding them accountable for teamwork can be particularly advantageous. For instance, a talented but challenging employee might lead a technical project, with an expectation to frequently engage with other team members. This method offers them a direct understanding of the value of constructive communication, encouraging gradual behavioral improvement.

A balanced approach that combines accountability with support is crucial. Offering challenging employees mentorship or coaching can be transformative, particularly when the mentor excels at navigating complex interpersonal dynamics. Mentors assist in developing interpersonal skills, establishing improvement goals, and serve as examples of productive behavior. The important factor is to match the employee with a mentor who exemplifies healthy communication, fosters accountability, and provides practical guidance. With time, mentorship can enhance self-management and emotional regulation, significantly diminishing disruptive behavioral tendencies.

Creating a culture centered around continuous feedback and improvement across the organization is among the most effective strategies for managing difficult personalities. A workplace that consistently engages in constructive feedback establishes an atmosphere of mutual respect and collective growth, thus diminishing the focus on any one individual's actions. When constructive criticism becomes standard practice, employees are less inclined to feel personally attacked, and challenging personalities are more likely to view feedback as part of their development rather than as punishment. By promoting a growth-oriented mindset throughout the organization, difficult employees can be motivated to enhance their behavior in a more supportive environment.

Your organization will also benefit from offering regular professional development opportunities that focus on interpersonal skills, emotional intelligence, and resilience. Workshops, training sessions, and seminars designed around self-awareness and communication equip employees with the tools they need to manage their behavior and enhance their interactions. Leaders should present these opportunities as advantageous for all, avoiding singling out specific individuals, which helps difficult personalities feel included rather than targeted. Over time, the skills learned through professional development can empower individuals to handle challenging situations more effectively, manage stress, and cultivate healthier relationships.

When problematic behavior continues despite efforts to address it, leaders should consider formal disciplinary measures as a final option. It's crucial to document every action taken, from initial feedback to coaching efforts, to ensure transparency and prevent misunderstandings. By placing disciplinary actions in the context of the organization's health and fairness, leaders can show that their decisions arise from a commitment to maintaining a positive work environment rather than from personal issues. Having clear, documented procedures for managing disruptive behavior also helps the organization stay consistent, fair, and legally safeguarded.

Effectively managing challenging personalities involves a combination of proactive strategies, empathetic dialogue, and organized interventions. Leaders should tackle each situation with patience and consistency, committed to maintaining the organization's standards. While it's important to recognize that not all difficult personalities may transform, their effects can be reduced through proper management. Finding a balance between empathy and accountability empowers leaders to create an environment where all employees feel respected, supported, and valued. By implementing these practical approaches, organizations can mitigate the effects of tough personalities and nurture a culture of collaborative growth.

Sometimes, one simple idea can transform a team, a workplace, or even an entire organization for the better.

Recognize, Mitigate, and Manage

A Guide to Improving Behavior in the Workplace

Toxic behaviors, as we all know, impede productivity, diminish morale, and generate stress and tension within the workplace. These detrimental behaviors usually develop slowly and can go undetected until they escalate and disrupt organizational harmony. If not addressed, they undermine trust, breed resentment, lower engagement, and contribute to a significant turnover of employees.

Have you ever seen a leader calmly navigate challenges in a way that made everyone around them feel capable and ready to grow?

Our final chapter summarizes some of the learning from what we have discussed to introduce a comprehensive checklist that enables managers and leaders to recognize toxic behaviors, understand their root causes, and implement strategic interventions to foster a healthier, more positive workplace culture. The following guidelines provide both warning signs of toxicity and actionable steps for mitigating its effects at different organizational levels.

Unchecked, toxic behaviors can originate from any part of an organization. Recognizing the signs at each level—individual, team, and organizational—enables a targeted approach to mitigation.

At an individual level, toxic behavior may appear as disrespect, resistance to collaboration, persistent negativity, or gossiping. Many do not recognize how their actions impact others, while some intentionally use such behavior to gain power or control. Warning signs include hesitance to join team efforts, evasion of accountability, and negative remarks that generate conflict. Other common indicators are emotional instability, defensiveness, and exaggerated responses to small issues. If left unaddressed, individually toxic behavior can escalate and spread to affect the larger team.

Toxicity at the team level frequently stems from unresolved conflicts, lack of trust, or the influence of a single negative individual whose behavior affects the group. Teams exhibiting toxic behaviors may experience breakdowns in communication, increased siloing, and a reduction in collaboration. These behaviors lead to a breakdown in group cohesion, ultimately impacting performance.

Organizational toxicity emerges due to systemic issues within company policies, leadership practices, or cultural norms. Signs of toxicity at this level may include a lack of transparency, ineffective communication, inconsistent standards, and, very often, a general atmosphere of mistrust. In toxic organizations, employees generally feel undervalued, and they almost always know they are unsupported. Both these sentiments contribute to low morale and high turnover. Unaddressed, organizational toxicity becomes deeply ingrained, and remediation often requires significant organizational changes. In the short term, these changes will be disruptive.

A Checklist for Mitigating Toxic Behaviors

A proactive approach is crucial for creating a positive work environment.

> *Just as a disease will not cure itself, corporate culture doesn't improve without positive interventions.*

Managers and leaders can use the following checklist to implement interventions designed to address and prevent toxic behaviors at all levels.

1. Develop a Clear Set of Behavioral Expectations and Values

Defining organizational values and behavioral expectations is foundational to creating a positive culture. Most impactfully, every single manager must model the behavior and, where possible, exceed expectations. Without the optimal behaviors being embraced and embodied by leadership, all discussion of corporate culture becomes toxic.

Establishing guidelines allows employees to understand what is considered acceptable and fosters accountability. However, although they should be common-sense based, values can't be imposed unilaterally and without explanation. Leaders must collaborate with teams to outline core values, such as respect, inclusivity, and teamwork, which should guide all interactions. Documenting and communicating these values helps ensure they become embedded within the organization. Additionally, aligning behavioral expectations with organizational values reinforces their importance.

When team members contribute to shaping these values, they are more likely to adhere to them. Consider implementing regular discussions or workshops that reinforce these behavioral standards, helping to foster an organizational culture that aligns with the values.

2. Identify and Address Toxic Behavior Early

Once toxic behaviors have been identified, addressing them promptly is essential. Managers should establish a safe, open-door policy that allows employees to voice concerns regarding workplace behaviors without fear of retaliation. When someone flags a toxic behavior, leaders must take it seriously, investigate the situation, and take the necessary steps to address it. This practice helps create an environment where team members feel supported and confident that any harmful behavior will be dealt with.

Addressing toxic behavior early involves listening to all parties involved, assessing the situation's impact, and providing constructive feedback. For many issues, one-on-one meetings where specific examples of the behavior, discussion of its impact, and corrective steps will result in tremendous gains. Most people want to do better, and often, they require proper guidance to improve. But even when the issue is recognized, it's rare when addressing the issue is a one-and-done matter. Judging progress fairly is not simple or binary.

In severe cases, termination or formal documentation and action plans may be required, ensuring the person understands the potential consequences if the behavior continues.

As a manager, you will deal with both straightforward and highly complex cases to address. Successfully remediated, the more complex ones can provide a tremendous source of accomplishment. But if the problematic individual refuses to improve, then despite your best efforts, they can be your greatest source of disappointment. Often, the challenge will be assessing whether they are making sufficient progress in their journey.

3. Encourage Open Communication

Open and transparent communication is the most effective way to combat toxicity. When people feel empowered to give and receive constructive feedback, they are more likely to resolve conflicts before they escalate.

It's not enough to simply talk about open communications. To be successful, leaders must prove people can speak their minds honestly and openly without fear of recrimination. If you attempt to create an open forum and punish anyone for communicating poorly, you are undermining your efforts and your corporate culture. Leaders can only promote a feedback culture by modeling it themselves, openly discussing their experiences, and encouraging team members to share ideas, concerns, and solutions without fear of judgment.

Leaders should make it a point to offer regular chances for feedback by hosting check-in meetings, sending out surveys, or facilitating team reflection sessions. Offering constructive feedback training can truly make a difference, empowering employees with the skills they need for healthy and respectful communication. By emphasizing open communication, organizations can nurture an environment where feedback is embraced as a valuable tool for growth, rather than a critique.

4. Foster Collaboration and Team Building

Toxic behavior often thrives in environments with limited camaraderie or poor team cohesion. In fact, in environments with strong camaraderie and a strong sense of ownership, a toxic outburst from a single team member is likely to fall on deaf ears.

Encouraging collaboration and building trust through team-building activities helps to prevent silos from developing and unhealthy competition. Managers can initiate team-building exercises, collaborative projects, or brainstorming sessions to promote unity and shared purpose. These activities allow team members to interact in relaxed, non-work settings, developing bonds that contribute to trust and mutual respect.

Team-building exercises should focus on developing empathy, active listening, and mutual understanding. For instance, conflict resolution workshops can improve how team members address disagreements and respect differences in communication styles. By investing in relationships within the team, organizations can foster an inclusive atmosphere where toxic behavior is less likely to flourish.

5. Implement Consistent Accountability Measures

Leaders should implement clear, consistent accountability measures to prevent inadvertently encouraging toxic behavior. This includes developing performance reviews, behavior evaluation protocols, and disciplinary actions aligned with the organization's values and policies. Transparent processes around accountability reassure employees that standards apply equally to everyone, discouraging harmful behaviors and promoting a culture of fairness.

When implementing new accountability measures, leaders need to articulate their intent clearly, highlighting that the aim is to foster a positive work environment rather than impose penalties. It's essential for leaders to make sure that all employees understand these policies and their application in everyday scenarios. Demonstrating transparency in enforcement ensures that everyone in the organization is subject to the same standard, reinforcing trust and fairness.

6. Provide Conflict Resolution Training and Support

It's imperative that managers accept that conflicts will be inevitable in any organization. Conflict resolution procedures and training are essential to help organizations manage these issues with the least amount of upheaval, because it's equally true that unresolved disputes will eventually fuel toxic behaviors.

While it would be nice for an entire organization to undergo conflict resolution training, this is not always practical. What is reasonable, however, is for all managers to participate in this form of training and demonstrate best practices to their colleagues and their direct reports. In doing so, each employee will observe the standards to which they need to aspire for promotion and learn the skills they need to handle disagreements productively.

Conflict management and resolution training is important and should focus on key areas like active listening, empathy, negotiation, and strategies to identify underlying issues. With these foundations, managers can be fully equipped to tackle challenges effectively. Training sessions are most beneficial when they include both individual and group workshops, encouraging employees to see conflict as a healthy part of collaboration rather than just a problem to avoid.

Organizations should also create a support system for employees to access during conflicts. Occasionally, employees feel unable to approach their manager, indicating a more significant issue. It's crucial for business leaders to have tools that notify them when such situations arise.

An independent whistleblower number sends a very strong message to the entire staff. If this reporting mechanism is ever used, management should thoroughly investigate any claims and consider designating conflict mediators or creating an internal task force skilled in conflict management to de-escalate any disputes and offer objective perspectives to all parties.

When management empowers employees with the correct tools to alert management to issues, management reinforces its commitment to honoring all voices equitably. When staff know that they are valued and their voices matter, it becomes much simpler to resolve conflicts respectfully and empathetically.

By demonstrating a professional approach, organizations can minimize friction and prevent the spread of toxic behavior.

7. Promote Recognition and Appreciation

A culture of sincere appreciation on the part of leadership toward all staff can go a long way toward counteracting the negative effects of toxic behavior, foster positivity, and enhance morale. Recognizing employees' contributions and successes validates their hard work and reinforces a sense of belonging.

Inevitably, there will be individuals who are Assholes in any organization. As discussed earlier in this book, there are both 'good' Assholes and toxic Assholes. While removing a bad Asshole from an organization becomes inevitable, reducing the appeal of toxic behavior on the part of anyone within the organization has to be a priority.

Leaders who make it a point to regularly express sincere gratitude to individuals and teams for their efforts, and who publicly acknowledge achievements and encourage peer recognition are verbally demonstrating their commitment to their teams. However, actions speak louder than words, and the teams also need to feel appreciated.

This can become difficult for some people when they are dealing with conflict. Again, this is where discerning the difference between an Asshole and a 'good' Asshole is key.

A good asshole, despite their poor approach and lack of proper communication skills, should be recognized as a canary in a coal mine, warning others of a significant business issue. They do not attack others on a personal level; they act out because they desire a superior performance. A toxic or bad Asshole, on the other hand, belittles others, and if they do not immediately remediate their behavior, they need to exit the organization.

Recognition of an individual's contributions does not need to be formal to be impactful; simple acknowledgments during meetings or written notes of appreciation can go a long way. Organizations can also create formal recognition programs, such as employee of the month awards or peer-nominated recognitions. Such gestures help cultivate an environment of encouragement where employees feel valued and motivated to maintain a constructive approach to their work.

8. Offer Access to Mental Health Resources

Most conflicts arise from misunderstandings or miscommunications. Staff in an organization want to deliver value and feel good about their accomplishments. Unaddressed stress and mental health issues are often at the root of conflict and toxic behaviors. An individual's negative response to an unwitting antagonist often reflects pre-existing issues that were triggered by a disconnect at work.

Providing access to mental health resources, such as counseling, workshops, and wellness programs, enables employees to manage personal challenges in a healthy, supported way and avoid transferring their issues to others. When organizations prioritize mental health, they do more than lower stress levels. They also de-escalate conflict and increase productivity. By helping staff members address the root causes of their behavior, a company creates an environment where employees feel safe, regardless of whether the issues affecting their lives stem from workplace stress, personal challenges, or burnout.

By making mental health resources readily available and promoting their use, management motivates employees to regard these tools as integral to the organization's support system. This approach allows managers to actively contribute to a culture that destigmatizes and normalizes seeking assistance, promotes open discussions about mental health, and provides flexible options for support. Such dedication to well-being minimizes the risk of toxic behavior and assists employees thrive.

9. Model Positive Behavior and Values at All Levels

Organizational leaders are powerful influencers within any workplace culture. When leaders model positive behaviors—such as respect, empathy, and transparency, they set a standard for the rest of the organization. By embodying these values and encouraging others to embrace similar standards, leaders create an atmosphere that discourages toxic behavior and encourages inclusivity.

While the absence of negativity will never be perfect, eliminating any toxicity should always be an ongoing priority. Dealing with these issues can never be shunted aside as something to address later. The most complicated issues are ongoing, as the personalities will inevitably be complex.

Although it's an ongoing process, managers must respond to any issues that arise and address any behavior that contradicts the core values. The failure to do so will lead to resentment and perceptions of favoritism.

Leadership modeling includes promoting a work-life balance, encouraging open communication, and remaining approachable. When employees witness positive behavior from the top, they are more likely to emulate it.

A key skill all employees can acquire from their leaders is conflict de-escalation. A manager who addresses problems with composure, listens to concerns, and thoroughly investigates underlying issues fosters greater long-term support compared to one who reacts impulsively and without thought.

When conflicts occur, some staff may wish for the proverbial hammer to come down hard on the colleague they are in conflict with. However, a manager's job is more complicated, and the repercussions of their decision will have a broader impact than simply resolving a single bilateral conflict.

When thinking about how to resolve conflicts, it's important for a manager to consider the whole organization, not just the two people involved. While there are certain boundaries that should always be respected, and some personal dislikes may linger, helping to ease conflicts allows managers to step into a mentoring role. By sharing insights on positive communication and conflict resolution and by nurturing the values they want to see flourish throughout the organization, managers can effectively help to calm most conflicts.

Managers may not like every team member equally, but to succeed, you do need to give every member the same level of respect. A failure to do so, will mean that you will ignore good advice from team members you feel less affinity toward over poor advice from one you like. Remember, while everyone will offer you their best advice and perspective, they do not always benefit from the same insights upon which to base their arguments.

Cultivating a Positive Workplace Culture

Addressing and mitigating toxic behavior requires commitment and consistency, but the benefits far outweigh the challenges. Organizations that prioritize a positive culture create environments where employees feel valued, supported, and motivated are infinitely more likely to succeed. Conversely, those that do not are doomed to fail.

A culture that actively discourages toxicity fosters innovation, collaboration, and mutual respect, enabling everyone to bring their best selves to work. Employees in positive workplaces report higher job satisfaction, better mental health, and greater loyalty, creating a foundation for long-term organizational success.

By proactively recognizing and addressing toxic behaviors, managers contribute to a healthier workplace and demonstrate that respect, empathy, and accountability are the cornerstones of their organization. This culture enhances productivity and strengthens employee bonds, enabling organizations to thrive.

Proactive leadership recognizes challenges early, and finds ways to turn them into opportunities for growth and collective success.

Final Thoughts

Thank you for reading this book. I trust that this collection of reflections has provided you with valuable insights that can help you avoid misjudging and mishandling any conflicts you face, now and in the future.

Whether the conflicts you are dealing with are professional or personal, they are challenging. We commonly feel that no one will understand the conflicts that rage within us. This is untrue. What we struggle with is our ability to objectively assess ourselves and the issues we are dealing with.

Helping others resolve conflict at work is an ongoing process. Your manager will make mistakes, even as they attempt to resolve issues. Judge the sincerity of their attempts and observe how they handle themselves. How they handle themselves is the clearest signal of how they will expect others to behave.

> *Have you ever left a project or workplace so inspired by the journey that you couldn't wait to take what you learned into your next adventure?*

My hope is that the lessons you pull from these essays helps you create that environment for others, and helps you learn from those experiences to expand your potential.

I highly recommend that everyone seek the counsel of others to help them assess the difficult situations they struggle with. Counseling can take many forms. It may involve talking to a therapist, or you may benefit from the insights of a mentor. No matter which route you feel is the appropriate choice today, please remember two important things: 1) Until you have a frank and honest talk with yourself regarding your own behavior and your role in any conflict, there will be no resolution; 2) if at first you don't succeed, try again. And again, and again, until you make progress.

Success comes from learning from failure, but it can never be achieved without failing first, and sometimes, failing often.

Anyone can talk about culture, but if you observe how a manager and leader comport themself and how they treat others, you will see that how they behave represents the authentic version of the culture that, inevitably, they will demand others to emulate.

Every interaction is an opportunity to build trust, foster growth, and leave a legacy of positivity and progress.

Thank-you!

www.ingramcontent.com/pod-product-compliance
Lightning Source LLC
Chambersburg PA
CBHW081144130726

47996CB00009B/2978